Having known Michae [barcode: MW00719091]
together in graduate s
as a dedicated leader, dynamic speaker,
author. *Riches Beyond Measure* is based on real-life experiences of real-life people. It's an ideal gift for pastors,
families, and friends. I highly recommend it.

—DR. CHARLES PAGE
PASTOR, FIRST BAPTIST CHURCH
CHARLOTTE, NORTH CAROLINA

Riches Beyond Measure is much like its author: inspirational, optimistic, practical, and full of good stories.
Michael Blackwell may be best known for his splendid
work putting children's lives back together, but he's also
fast becoming known as a prolific author with some
important observations about the way we live our lives
and the principles for which we stand.

—JACK BETTS
ASSOCIATE EDITOR, *THE CHARLOTTE OBSERVER*

Riches Beyond Measure is a collection of simple stories
with profound meaning. Although brief enough to be
read in one sitting, I found the book to be more effec-
tive by reading one chapter a day, allowing the nuggets
of truth enough time to sink in.

—PHILLIP J. KIRK, JR.
PRESIDENT, NORTH CAROLINA CITIZENS
FOR BUSINESS & INDUSTRY

Riches Beyond Measure delivers what it promises—a con-
cise guide to shaping a life worth living. Michael Blackwell's fresh and original insights provide a blueprint for
creating the kind of life you know you were meant to
live. A valuable resource based on spiritual wisdom and
biblical principles.

—MARCIA FORD
AUTHOR OF *MEMOIR OF A MISFIT*
AND *101 MOST POWERFUL PROMISES IN THE BIBLE*

I enjoy books that help me see more than I can see in myself. *Riches Beyond Measure* is such a book, and Michael Blackwell is such an author. You will find immediate benefits from the book to help you be your best. *Riches Beyond Measure* is a fresh breeze for any life that may need one.

—FLOYD A. CRAIG
PRESIDENT, CRAIG COMMUNICATIONS
NASHVILLE, TENNESSEE

Riches Beyond Measure, by dynamic speaker and author Michael Blackwell, is an inspirational and motivational book. It shows readers, in twelve steps, ways they can lead and live a better life. You will embrace and celebrate your own personal riches as a result of reading this book.

—SHARON ALLRED DECKER
PRESIDENT, TANNER COMPANIES
RUTHERFORDTON, NORTH CAROLINA

Riches Beyond Measure is a guide, amazing in its simplicity, that helps direct people toward making the most of the life they have been given, no matter what talents they were born with.

—KAREN PARKER
WINSTON-SALEM JOURNAL

RICHES BEYOND MEASURE

DR. MICHAEL BLACKWELL
WITH KEN WALKER

CREATION HOUSE PRESS

A STRANG COMPANY

RICHES BEYOND MEASURE
by Dr. Michael Blackwell with Ken Walker
Published by Creation House Press
A Strang Company
600 Rinehart Road
Lake Mary, Florida 32746
www.creationhousepress.com

Unless otherwise noted, all Scripture quotations are from the Holy Bible, New International Version. Copyright © 1973, 1978, 1984, International Bible Society. Used by permission.

Cover design by Terry Clifton

Library of Congress Control Number: 2004109823
International Standard Book Number: 1-59185-642-6

04 05 06 07 08 — 987654321
Printed in the United States of America

I would like to dedicate *Riches Beyond Measure* to four congregations that played a pivotal role in my ultimate career path:

- Flint-Groves Baptist Church, Gastonia, North Carolina

- Ridge Road Baptist Church, Raleigh, North Carolina

- First Baptist Church, Carthage, North Carolina

- Monument Heights Baptist Church, Richmond, Virginia

The first church is where I spent my childhood and youth. The remaining three offered me gainful employment after I graduated from seminary and before I became president of the Baptist Children's Homes of North Carolina. Together these churches provided me true riches beyond measure and set me on a path of lifelong service.

Acknowledgments

WHAT FUN I had researching the ideas for *Riches Beyond Measure!* The journey became an adventure in discovery because of my close collaboration with Ken Walker. Thanks, Ken, for not only your assistance, but also your friendship. Ken and I both have prayed that this little book will bring hope, encouragement, and inspiration to those who read it. We agree that without the dedication of Jennie Counts, bringing this book to fruition would have posed a much more challenging task. Jennie is my executive assistant (official title: Executive Vice President, Administration, Baptist Children's Homes of North Carolina) and friend who offered numerous suggestions that strengthened this material. Thanks, Jennie, for your patience, diligence, and hard work

I am also grateful to the Broyhill Family Foundation of Lenoir, North Carolina, whose assistance has enabled us to embark on widespread distribution of *Riches Beyond Measure.* Finally, Ken and I both thank our families for their unfailing support of whatever impossible dream we set out to accomplish.

—DR. MICHAEL C. BLACKWELL
THOMASVILLE, NORTH CAROLINA

Contents

Chapter 1

Step 1: Accept Yourself

I RENEWED ACQUAINTANCES WITH old friends at my fortieth high school reunion—an automatic clue that I am no spring chicken. But there is something special about making it this far. Four decades after high school, everyone has shed youthful pretenses. Nobody has anything left to prove. People are much more mellow when they are not trying to show off. Generally, we were laid-back, glad to be alive, and happy to see each other.

Among the folks I enjoyed chatting with was Walter, also a classmate during my four years at the University of North Carolina in Chapel Hill. A successful banker who recently retired after thirty-four years in his field, Walter has been crippled with polio since age five. I still remember his courageous climbing of the steep steps of our four-story high school (this was long before laws required accessibility to public buildings for those with physical problems.)

He could have easily become embittered, but Walter maintained a philosophical outlook about his disability, even after measures to correct it provided meager improvement. During the summer of our sophomore year, he faced spinal fusion surgery, but it was canceled. He wound up wearing a heavy cast, which caused him to start his junior year a month late. Though walking stiffly and leaning heavily to the left, he kept plodding along with a smile on his face. Our class elected him its "Unsung Hero."

Because he could walk only short distances, in college administrators reluctantly allowed him to drive a golf cart around campus. We constantly kidded him about his special privileges. As you can imagine, the reunion brought forth rich memories of those times, as well as the pranks we used to play. The friendship that several others and I had with him was so strong that once we swiped his golf cart, just so we could watch his expression when he ambled out of his dormitory. Yes, that was an unkind thing to do, but we thought it was funny. So did Walter.

As we chuckled over those times, Walter stopped and pointed at several high school buddies who had experienced college life with him. Getting a bit misty-eyed, he said, "One of the best things that ever happened to me was you guys. When something happens like what happened to me, you know your true friends. I did not want to have polio, but without it I probably would never have known the love I've discovered—or the closeness to God it has brought."

Chills still caress my spine when I recall that night. For me, Walter embodies the definition of courage. He could have said, "My dreams have been broken so there must not be a God. I'm going to be an agnostic and go through life with bitterness for what has happened to me." But he didn't. Instead, he kept his faith, prayed, followed God's will, and saw life as a gift. Most of all, by accepting who he was and the hand he had been dealt, he could walk forward, no matter how halting his steps.

TOWARD A BETTER LIFE

Accept yourself. This is the first step toward a better life. We are human; therefore, we have limits. We come up against new problems or challenges and recognize that we have weaknesses. Think back over the past week. If we are honest, we will recognize that we likely have offended someone, spoken harshly in a moment of pressure or irritation, or made questionable decisions. We did not mean to take such missteps, yet they happened.

Such mistakes not only upset our internal compass, they provide rich fodder for our enemies. Affected by others' opinions of us, we can easily (and meekly) accept their biting criticisms, second-guessing, or harsh judgments. Sometimes others speak or act as though they do not think we are very important, sending us into a self-pitying mode. Or, because someone else has more material riches, education, or social standing, we devalue our own worth.

Many of the roots of self-deprecation sprout from childhood. When we first learn about life and do not know enough to form opinions, we go by the opinions of others—parents, other adults, or more mature siblings. If such people treat us as unimportant because of our small stature, it can plant the thought that we are small and unimportant. Sadly, some adults never overcome this misguided, childish outlook.

Yet, despite all that may come against us, one thing that should reassure us is God's love. God accepts each of us as people of value and worth, simply because He loves us. This is the kind of love we have craved throughout our lives. It is the kind of love that does not stop when we do something wrong, or wither and die because we made a mistake. If God accepts us for who we are rather than because of our actions, good looks, or special abilities, then we should be able to accept ourselves.

Finding our "self," knowing our identity, and not letting it deter us from moving on is one of the secrets to success. Famed author James Michener spoke of this in *The Fires of Spring*: "For this is the journey that men make, to find themselves. If they fail in this, it doesn't matter much what else they find. Money, fame, position, many loves, revenge—all are of little consequence. And when the tickets are collected at the end of the ride they are tossed into a bin marked failure. But if a man happens to find himself—if he knows what he can be depended upon to do, the limits of his courage, the position from which he will no longer retreat…the extent of his dedication…then he has found a mansion which he can inhabit with dignity all the days of his life."[1]

Carlyle Marney, a friend from Charlotte who has since passed on, once told about a man he knew who cracked up emotionally. It cost him everything he had. The victim's life literally disintegrated, dragging down his marriage, personal life, and professional achievements. What was at the heart of his troubles? He never made up his mind who he was and where he stood. Quipped Marney, "He didn't have any sideboards to his wagon. Whatever way the road leaned, he spilled his load."

DEALING WITH TRAGEDY

Accepting oneself includes accepting setbacks and tragedies that are inevitable facts of life. At the same reunion where I saw Walter, I met up with another old friend who became an oncologist. As we talked, we agreed that our work has much in common. I oversee a network of children's homes that try to salvage wounded lives. He attempts to salvage whatever time can be gained from a disease that, despite modern medical advances, sometimes represents a death sentence.

"I see two kinds of people in my office," this doctor told me. "Those who are embittered and destroyed by illness, and those who are ennobled by it. Some people become angry when they learn they are going to die. They lash out at God and everybody around them. Everything centers on them and what is happening to them.

"Others are the opposite. They get in touch with the ground of their beliefs, with some deep faith inside of themselves. They become peaceful centers of radiant hope and goodness. They become more loving and considerate of others. They submit themselves to the will of God."

Prominent Swiss physician and psychiatrist Paul Tournier gave me great insight on how accepting oneself can spell the difference between a victorious life and one lived in shallow misery. In *The Meaning of Persons* he told a story of two patients.[2]

The first was a highly successful politician whose appeal and charisma had carried him to a string of victories at the ballot box. Though outwardly full of charm and confidence, his private actions revealed a much different nature. He confessed feeling so timid that his hands shook violently whenever he shared a cup of tea with a small group of friends.

The second patient was a forty-year-old man who felt so insecure that his mother accompanied him to the office. Nervous and fidgety, he sat on the edge of his chair throughout their initial interview. However, over time, doctor and patient developed a basic trust. To his surprise, Dr. Tournier discovered the soul of an adventurer. Though the man dreamed of heroism, daring deeds, and voyages to distant lands, he was ineffectual. Because he had not accepted himself and embraced the idea of taking action to realize those dreams, he remained tied to his mother by an invisible cord.

Accepting self means we not only achieve our dreams, but also help others reach theirs. We do this not by writing a best-selling book, becoming a famed motivational speaker, or selling a million videos on "The Successful Life." No, we inspire others to greatness simply by seeing them as people of worth and value. Life runs at its best when people treat each other with honor and respect. Poor relationships with others injure both parties' feelings. It dims all hopes of success in businesses, friendships, cooperative ventures, and families.

The one who treats people poorly suffers in other ways. A man or woman constantly at odds with others reaps a harvest of loneliness, or at best a grudging acceptance in professional circles. The pain may simply be felt inside, with the individual ill at ease with self. By hurting others, such people hurt themselves. Do other people speak unkindly, make dumb moves, and fail in their endeavors? Sure. But so do you. Love means making allowances for others' shortcomings, just as they make allowances for ours.

To complete this picture of acceptance, I offer the word *comfort*. Be comfortable with your body, your spirit, and with others.

- *Be comfortable with your body.* Do you find yourself frequently wishing your body were a different type, size, shape, or color? To be at peace with your body requires a "faith-full" acceptance of your body type. Most people cannot be supremely shapely or muscular. Yet, most of us can develop the awareness that our body is not something to fight, but to accept and value. Because of its intricate nature and creation, it is a thing of beauty. Comfort involves acceptance.

- *Be comfortable with your spirit.* Many dwell on our incompleteness, sinfulness, and faults. That is self-defeating behavior. You will never know the joy God intended for you to have if you stay mired in the quicksand of negative, defeatist thinking. Sure, periodically we all struggle with fears and anxieties, but we must remember each of us came into the world with the possibility of wholeness and completeness. While that is a lifelong quest, we can take comfort in knowing that we are not alone in our journey. The One who was with us in the beginning will be with us to the end.

- *Be comfortable with others.* This is the fruit of the previous pair of comforts. The person at comfort with his or her body and spirit has no compulsion to lash out at others. Those who are comfortable with their body and spirit no longer need to project their discomfort onto the world or onto others. They no longer need to hate, discriminate, or hurt others.

Acceptance = comfort. There is a right way to order our lives so they are not constantly tangled and adrift, but moving forward with shape and aim. Our level of comfort plays a huge part in how we view the world and live in it. We are not totally mature unless we know the comfort for which we have been created and intended.[3]

Chapter 2

Step 2: Seek Help

THEY LOOKED LIKE the all-American family: Jim, the smiling, smartly-dressed pastor of a loving church and his wife, a concerned mother. The guidance and care they provided for their only son, Matt, shone through in his pleasant demeanor and above-average grades in school.

But this picture of happiness crumbled as their son turned the corner from adolescence. Gradually, Matt's teenage behavior deteriorated. Not only did his grades drop with a thud, but he also became angry and violent, lashing out at his mother and other students. Stressed out, Sandra felt relieved on occasions when he left the house, mumbling, "I'm going to see a friend." Of course, had she known that the friend happened to be her son's marijuana supplier, her peace would have flared into panic.

Despite Matt's efforts to hide the truth, it became too blatant to ignore. Afraid for their son's safety, concerned for what his future held, and overcoming the fear of what their congregation might say, Jim and Sandra sought help. They took him to a boys' camp operated by our network of children's homes. There they learned that it was not just Matt who had a problem. The whole family had to resolve the issues that had torn them apart.

Like other residents, Matt checked in with a load of emotional and behavioral baggage that was too heavy to lug around at home. He would spend the next two years releasing those feelings as he canoed hundreds of miles, backpacked to remote areas, and swam in rivers, lakes, and the ocean.

Soon after Matt checked in, a social worker discovered the source of his anger. When Matt was a toddler, his father had a drug problem, which caused a marital separation. Although his father overcame his addiction, turned to God, and reconciled his marriage, the scars remained. As Matt grew older, he also grew further apart from Jim. Like his father, he struggled to control his temper.

It took the passage of time coupled with intense personal effort and numerous counseling sessions to reconcile the family. Father and son learned how to agree and disagree. Sandra saw her role in the situation, explaining, "We think as parents, 'Camp will fix the boys and send them home when they are finished,' but it doesn't work that way. We told Matt, 'It's not just you; we are all going to set goals.' We all had something to learn."

Though this story is still being written, it is headed in the right direction. Matt has returned home. He and his father enjoy fishing together, building model airplanes, and working on the goals they set earlier. But this improved state of affairs could easily have ended in disaster. His parents could have allowed fears of damaged pride, inconvenience, or possible social reprisals to bottle up the truth. Sooner or later, ignoring brewing trouble is like lighting a stick of dynamite.

Yet, I know this happens constantly. I have seen the fallout. One woman, who spent her teenage years in one of our cottages, had lived in absolute filth before coming to us. Animals camped out inside her home, which had no sanitation facilities. When social service workers visited to investigate a complaint, they condemned the house—literally. The county later burned it to the ground.

Both the conditions and what followed posed one of the ugliest situations I have ever encountered. When Heather came to live at the children's home, her self-esteem and will to live had evaporated. She trusted no one. Her parents had disowned her for revealing family secrets. Not surprisingly,

Heather had to be hospitalized after attempting suicide.

Fortunately, she overcame her circumstances. At first, this young woman knew nothing of personal hygiene, which meant the staff had to start from scratch. Abused in the past, she did not want anyone to touch her (especially a man). It took a year before she accepted the staff's love. But in the end, Heather survived. After several years in her group home, she had become socially active, made the high school honor roll, and graduated with a fine academic record. Later she became a childcare worker.

Heather succeeded. But what of her parents? I do not know. I grieve for the damage to their lives. Who knows what terrible circumstances lay in their background, leading them to live in such squalor? Yet, had they stopped and asked for help, perhaps they could have avoided the crisis that led to a broken family.

RELUCTANT SEEKERS

While this is an extreme example, it underscores the reluctance of people to seek help for emotional, psychological, family, or marital problems. Always trying to put on a happy face, they retreat into a state of denial. While denial can help one temporarily cope with harsh circumstances, it is foolish to pitch a tent in Never-Never Land.

One of society's most damaging trends is the plague of divorce, now so common that a thirty-something has written a book on starter marriages. She was referring to young people's habit of hopping in and out of supposed long-term relationships in five years or less.

Of course, the roots of this problem go back for decades. Earlier in my career, I regularly counseled couples with troubled marriages—or at least I tried. I cannot count how many times a marriage was on the rocks and one party (usually the husband) would say, "Ah, I don't need that. If she wants to go, that's fine, but I'll just gut it out." Although my doctoral studies emphasized counseling, one man said, "Well, you know, I just feel you're too young." That was just a convenient excuse to ignore the situation. When I needed major dental surgery recently, I would have been foolish to leave the office because the dentist was only thirty years old.

Sadly, divorce seems to be tightening its ugly grip on our society, when many marriages could be salvaged if the couple would just ask for help. While there are numerous factors behind divorce, a leading problem is communication. When these channels get clogged, the match is in trouble. It reminds me of a cartoon I saw once that showed a husband and wife sitting together at the breakfast table, sipping coffee. The wife was thinking, "Our marriage is in trouble. We had better talk about it." The husband was thinking, "Our marriage is in trouble. I had better keep my mouth shut."

No matter what the problem, take time to discuss it with a trusted friend, confidant, counselor, or other adviser. Seeking help is a sign of strength, not weakness. In recent decades, society has made progress at getting past the macho, all-American embrace of pride and self-reliance. Still, we have not conquered the problem. Too many people lead lives of quiet desperation. They get out of bed, go to work, breathe, and eat, but life holds little meaning, joy, or fulfillment.

Sometimes, getting to the next level, whether in a job, a marriage, a relationship, or even just a hobby, takes more resources than you possess. So why not seek out those who can help instead of turning away from them? You would not try to set a broken arm at home with an old tree limb for a splint or operate on yourself to remove a ruptured appendix. Nor should you allow personal problems to afflict you like migraine headaches. Look for those who can help you overcome them.

Healthy Outlook

None of us is immortal. Yet millions die from heart disease, clogged arteries, diabetes, cancer, and other diseases that could have been successfully treated, or at least slowed, adding precious years to their lives. Generally, I have observed that people are more willing to deal with physical problems than mental or emotional ones. Yet some wander blindly down the path of obesity, smoking, or carrying an overload of stress, never consulting a doctor or recognizing that preventive medicine beats hospital recuperation.

I received my mid-course correction more than twenty-five years ago, when my heart started beating so fast I thought that I was having a heart attack. A healthy, thirty-six-year-old jogger, I could not believe this was happening. Looking back, I am convinced it stemmed from stress. Occupational irritations had me in an agitated state when I arrived at the hotel where I had booked a two-night stay during a convention.

Back then, if someone wanted to spend an extra night in a hotel, they could, regardless of who else was coming. When I got to the desk and told them I had a reservation, the clerk said, "I'm sorry, we're full." He then directed me to another hotel several miles away, a major inconvenience since I had picked this one for its proximity to the meeting. Steam figuratively rose from my ears as I quickly contemplated this unexpected development.

Suddenly my heart started racing like a car in the Indianapolis 500. I felt a bit dizzy, but fortunately maintained consciousness. Catching my breath and going as fast as the law would allow, I drove to the same hospital where both of our children were born. Striding into the emergency room, I gasped, "I think I'm having a heart attack!" In what seemed like a few minutes, they had me in a bed, heavily sedated.

This represented a watershed moment for me. While I cannot say that my life flashed before my eyes, or that it made me incredibly aware of my mortality, I came face to face with the reality that I cannot control everything. A physical crisis can also pose a crisis of the spirit. Lying there after I regained consciousness, I thought, "Is there something wrong with me?

What about my family? What will happen to them if I'm not around to help our children?"

No longer could I take my health for granted. I had sailed on for years, seldom seeing a doctor except for a serious cold or nagging bout of the flu. And bam! I was hospitalized for three days. During that time I realized I had to slow down and stop treating everything like a matter of life and death. Two years later I read a study that said caffeine was a prime contributor to my condition, known as tachycardia. That promptly ended my coffee-drinking days.

I would like to say that solved the problem, but it took ten years to bring it under control. After the initial crisis, I had to seek emergency room treatment several more times and once had to be hospitalized. The day I checked out, I spoke to a large audience, but stepped into and out of that meeting gingerly. A small, sudden movement could have sparked my overstressed heart back into action.

I finally wound up getting an echocardiogram to see whether they could pinpoint the source of the trouble. Doctors considered doing surgery to clip a device inside my chest that would correct the malfunction in my body's electrical system. In a sense, life changed forever. My jogging days ended. The preciousness of life and its treasures—such as my wife, family, and friends—took on new significance.

Looking back on the first time this happened, I fondly remember those in our small community who greeted me after I was released amid a rumor that I had had a heart attack. As they gathered around to hear my explanation that this was not quite the case, smiles, concern, and love shone on their faces. In that instant, I realized that people have an intrinsic need for love and to express love. One of the ways they do that is by helping others in time of need. When you reach out to seek that help, you are blessing them with a spiritual connection. Such treasure ought to be valued highly.

Chapter 3

Step 3: Be a Friend

Dᴜʀɪɴɢ Wᴏʀʟᴅ Wᴀʀ II, some American soldiers took their buddy's body to a cemetery. But a priest stopped them, saying, "You can't bury your friend here if he's not a Catholic." Discouraged but not defeated, they buried their fellow soldier just outside the cemetery fence. But when they came to pay their respects the next morning, they couldn't find the grave. When they questioned the priest, he said, "The first part of the night I stayed awake, disturbed by what I had told you. The second part of the night I spent moving the fence."[1]

As an only child, I can identify with that story. Though loved by my parents, I sometimes fantasized about having a brother who could show me the kind of care those soldiers did for their fallen comrade. I daydreamed of sharing camaraderie, building tree houses, and slaying dragons together. I just never knew it would take until my mid-thirties to find him. Nor did I expect that he would be ten years younger.

Tim and I met at a conference twenty-five years ago. Captivated by a talk I delivered, he visited my room afterward to tell me, "You're an outstanding speaker." Anyone who has gripped a podium knows that such a compliment can boost the ego. But in this case there was genuine admiration rather than flattery. Later that year, I returned the favor by going to hear him speak and compliment him on his abilities. The next year, I was an usher in his wedding.

Not long after that, our professional paths placed us in the same city, where our friendship blossomed. We talked two or three times a week, often meeting for breakfast at Aunt Sarah's Pancake House. When our occupations sent us in divergent directions, we still maintained weekly contact. I have called him from England; he has phoned me from Israel.

We share many similarities, among them education, goals, likes and dislikes, an interest in leadership, politics, a sense of humor—even our "broad" physiques. Yet, where he is gregarious, ambitious, and meticulous, I am more laid-back and spontaneous. I do not necessarily like everything he does, and vice versa. But that is part of friendship. We allow each other to be our true selves, without criticizing or trying to reform the other. We accept that we are part of the human family, with innate weaknesses.

I have often said that if a person's face lights up when I walk into the room, then I can do anything. No matter what obstacles I am facing, no matter the pressures or criticisms I just encountered, such a glow makes me feel like a rich man. Naturally, my spouse offers that kind of support. But a friend adds another dimension to life. Tim and I know we will always be there for each other. We can say anything to each other, knowing the comment will go no further. We also share joy, sometimes laughing so hard that we wonder if we will lose our breath.

When I celebrated fifteen years as president of our childcare agency, Tim showed up to warm my heart with these words: "We simply cannot wholesale our most intimate hopes, fears, thoughts, and feelings to a lot of people. That is reserved for only a few—a spouse and maybe one or two others. Henry Adams was right: 'One friend in a lifetime is much, two are many, three are hardly possible.' And for me, one of those is Mickey.

"I wish I could communicate the inexpressive comfort of feeling secure with a person, having neither to weigh thoughts nor measure words, but to pour them all out, just as they are, wheat and chaff together, knowing that a good hand will take and sift the wheat and keep what is worth keeping. And then, with a loving hand, blow the rest away."

THE SPIRIT OF FRIENDSHIP

Yet friendship means more than laughs and warm fuzzies at banquets. When Tim's mother died (and they were very close), he maintained his composure until I arrived at the funeral home. Then he collapsed in my arms, sobs wracking his body, as if he could not let loose until his buddy appeared. I knew how he felt the night he gently walked to my side as I gazed at my father in a casket. Not knowing Tim was coming, my emotions exploded.

Friendship takes dedication. Millions of marriages have fallen apart because they were not nurtured; a similar fate can befall friends. They must grow, accommodate, forgive, and move on, always with an appreciation for this relationship's unique nature. For at its heart, friendship contains a spiritual element. There is a force beyond ourselves that blends people into friends and then keeps the friendship alive.

Friends are those people who will risk their comfort, safety, convenience, and feelings to help us, comfort us, and do their best to ensure we receive the best life has to offer. While this may sound trivial or pedestrian, America's leading social indicators show that it is not. In *Bowling Alone*, Harvard University professor Robert Putnam traced the decline in our nation's "social capital" from 1975 to 2000.[2]

Including charts that graphically display the problem, his book shows how decreasing citizen participation affects everything from our political system to a host of civic and community organizations. Putnam identifies various factors for this decline, such as pressures of time and money, metropolitan sprawl, electronic entertainment (especially television), and generational changes. But what caught my eye was this comment from sociologist Claude S. Fischer: "Social networks are important in all of our lives, often for finding jobs, more often for finding a helping hand, companionship, or a shoulder to cry on."[3]

Since the author spells out a plan for increasing social involvement in the first decade of the twenty-first century, I am not trying to replicate his extensive research. But I would suggest that rekindling community within our socially impoverished society starts with being a friend.

I picture community as the spokes of a wheel, starting in the center with family and extending outward to close friends, social groups, neighborhoods, and professional relationships. Each has its strengths and weaknesses; each adds flavoring that spices up life, and a shortage in one area diminishes another.

In the midst of affluence that has given us creature comforts beyond the imagination of most of the world—but has also stimulated endless cravings for more, and created the modern corporate scandals that captured national headlines—I fear we have lost sight of the value of friendship. There are vast, intangible qualities offered by human relationships that enrich us in ways that money cannot.

Former presidential speechwriter Peggy Noonan touched on this in her memoir about life at the White House, noting the modern, bottom-line orientation that led national television networks to cut loose veteran reporters. With keen insight, she noted how corporate moguls failed to understand that keeping a great man on the payroll past his prime creates the greatest impact on his coworkers.

"They realize the company cares about them in a careless world, and they decide to care about the company," she wrote. "And so they come up with their share of the bargain and—I could pick from many examples—decide, as the correspondent Bruce Dunning did, to fight his way onto the last plane out of Da Nang, where he huddled on the floor and kept his tape recorder rolling and reported live as the plane barely made it up, as desperate people fell from the wheels. He didn't stop talking, and you could hear the terror of what was happening through the terror of his shaking voice. There has never been a better moment in broadcast journalism."[4]

Friends inspire us, encourage us, teach us, and lead us to great achievements. When her mentor from her early days in journalism died, syndicated columnist Ellen Goodman wrote of basking in the glow of knowing that he was on her side. One of the things she treasured most was when *Boston Globe* editor Tom Winship sent her notes praising something she had written: "Most of us kids are well into middle-age now, but I say without embarrassment that I still have my stash of his 'tiger notes,' the scribbled words that he would send when you wrote something that tickled him. Tell the management gurus and the corporate incentive honchos and the stock-option makers, I worked for those notes."[5]

MORE THAN ACQUAINTANCES

I know the joy of such professional associations, including one that has endured for nearly fifty years. Consisting of a fluid group of up to two dozen professionals who meet each month for lunch, original organizers invited men from a range of backgrounds to ensure "wrangling" during these wide-ranging discussions. Hence, the name, "The Wranglers."

We discuss everything, be it politics, social ethics, current events, the frustrations of life in the public eye, or inspiring books. Jokes flow as freely as the iced tea—such as the pastor who recalled putting his hands in his pocket during a sermon and watching with dismay as his zipper split down the middle. But personal concerns always take first place on the agenda. Members are not immune from life's maladies, be that fatal illnesses, divorce, or the grief of losing family members and friends.

"It's a place where we feel accepted and don't have to perform to be accepted," says Tom, an executive with a charitable foundation. "People have found understanding about the stress facing their family without being judged. I think of it as a private church. There's a measure of grace that comes through the private church that doesn't always come through the public one."

They are the kind of people he can call at 3 a.m., and who have called him when they heard of his personal struggles. Mentioning how the Wranglers are the kind of guys who will be there when you get sick, Tom adds a comment that underscores the value of the social capital Putnam discusses: "There are a lot of guys you don't want at the hospital because they haven't invested themselves in you."

These are also the kind of men who will drive more than two hours each way to attend a two-hour meeting. Ken, a pastor from Raleigh, North Carolina, echoes Tom's comment about the unconditional love he senses, calling the gatherings an "oasis" in his life. He says, "If one of us shares something that is an accomplishment, no one thinks he is bragging. If one of us shares something that is difficult, no one thinks he is complaining."

Still, there is a twinge of sadness associated with our group. One senior participant laments the general aging of our numbers, which he believes points to the waning of social and professional intimacy. In today's rushed society, gathering to exchange views has lost its glitter; he recalls the younger man who told him, "Your generation is the last of the nurturers. When you go off the scene, there won't be anyone to carry it on."

I do not take quite as pessimistic a view. For one, in his book Putnam recalls how a similar shortage of social involvement in the late 1800s stimulated the formation of dozens of organizations, from the Gideons and the Veterans of Foreign Wars to the Lions Club, Rotary, and Jaycees. In addition, deep within the human soul lies the need for close human contact, for friends who appreciate us in spite of our foibles and follies.

As Tony, one of the newer members of the Wranglers, says of another close network of friends, "My life has been enriched by people who have been part of it. I don't ever feel fully alone. There are half a dozen guys I know I can call, and they'll stop what they're doing [to help me]. Just having that knowledge adds a great deal of security to your life."

This is the kind of security that will follow you to the end of your days, nourishing your soul with a pearl of great price: presence. People who will be there when your child dies in an accident, your spouse suffers from a fatal disease, or your career has just come crashing down amid forces beyond your control can usually be numbered on one hand—two at most. Cherish such treasures. Be a friend.

Chapter 4

Step 4: Love Abundantly

WARD AND NELL Mullis made an unlikely couple. He stood well over six feet tall; she barely reached five feet. He was as outgoing as she was shy and reserved. Yet, during their marriage they were inseparable. When he checked his bride of nearly forty-nine years into the hospital, he shuddered over the possibility of spending their golden anniversary alone.

Three days later, after extensive surgical exploration, the doctors delivered the news: Nell did not have stomach cancer. It was worse. She had a cancerous tumor in her stomach that had grown through the small intestine. The hideous growth had attached itself to the pancreas and other tissue in such a way that it could not be surgically removed.

About three weeks after she was first hospitalized, Nell came home. Soon, she underwent the first of twenty-eight radiation treatments, continuing at a rate of four per week. Ultimately, the harsh therapy rendered her bedridden. Ward faced a decision either to employ nurses to watch after his wife while he tended to his commercial real estate business or stay with her. Their children thought he should take some time away from the house. In addition, his partners needed some kind of decision regarding his availability.

The choice came easily. He would stay at home with Nell. That meant such tasks as bathing her and connecting her feeding tube to a machine every night so she could receive liquid nutrients. While some might consider that an unbearable strain, Ward did not. Just as his wife had been a wonderful person throughout their marriage, she made a wonderful patient, he told me. She never complained about her plight, and matter-of-factly explained which dress she preferred for burial and where friends could send memorial donations.

After knowing this gregarious supporter of our network of child care facilities for years, it was hard enough listening to this painful story. Finally, I lost my composure when he explained his decision to stay home in a halting, highly emotional voice: "There will always be high-rise buildings to buy and sell. But there is only one Nell."

I count it a privilege to know men such as Ward, who demonstrate that the idea of sticking by one's mate will never grow old. During their time together, they never spent one night apart because one of them had their "nose out of joint." They never forgot a birthday, wedding anniversary, or other special occasion until her death. Ward still has the first Valentine's Day card Nell ever sent him when he was in the Marines.

More than a year into this emotionally draining routine, when anyone would have understood Ward's nerves wearing thin amid brewing cabin fever, he remained gracious. "Nell and I have enjoyed a wonderful relationship in our marriage, and we have not lost sight of the many things we have to be thankful for, such as our love and devotion to one another," he says, listing such blessings as:

- Their faith in Christ;

- A wonderful family of three children, six grandchildren, and two great-grandchildren;

- A host of caring, helpful friends;

- The good health that enabled him to be a full-time caregiver;

- That taking time off from work would not create a financial crisis: "Circumstances are just not always that way."

ENDURING TO THE END

Love, faithfulness, caring, commitment, and tenderness are summed up in the phrase "Till death do us part." Love endures to the end, never giving up, walking away, or forsaking those who have done so much for you and meant so much to your life. It truly conquers all. Love is a powerful need for each human being, with a powerful impact—not only on those who give and receive it, but also in those who observe it.

Jack Dossenbach, a former trustee of our organization, proved the value of faithfulness when his first wife was diagnosed with Alzheimer's disease. Her illness lingered for fifteen long and sometimes painful years. After several years of having a woman visit regularly to do housework and help tend to Sadie's needs, Jack surrendered to the inevitable.

But he did not forget Sadie Leigh after placing her in a nursing home. Twice a day, every day for a decade, he went to visit. A half-hour in the morning, then for sixty to ninety minutes in the evening, when he fed her supper to make sure she ate a good meal. Although he couldn't converse with her, just being by her side strengthened his faith.

"My goodness, she was the mother of my children," says Jack if you ask why it was important that he kept such a strung-out vigil. "And I know it was important for our children to see me being faithful. They have told me that and written letters to that effect."

Their ten grandchildren were touched as well. After Jack wrote his memoirs as a gift to his family, his granddaughter, Beth, wrote to say how she had always admired him for being such a good father, husband, and grandfather. "My head swelled even more with pride when I realized the legacy of love and faith that you have given your family. You are an inspiration to me. I'll be so happy and proud to have you at my wedding."

But that is not the end of Jack's story. About six months after his wife died—as a courtesy—he invited his former pastor's widow to a groundbreaking ceremony for one of our children's homes. She had been alone for ten years after her husband died of cancer. As it turned out, that outdoors ceremony, held in sub-freezing weather, was the setting where Cupid shot his arrow into both their hearts. As the crowd huddled around fires during my speech at the ceremony, Nancy moved closer to Jack for warmth. She hoped I would stop speaking soon, while Jack hoped I would keep talking.

The following spring they married, giving each other support and comfort in their golden years. Neither will forget their first mate, but they are grateful for the love they share. "There was a reason for it to work out the way it did," Jack says, reflecting on all those years when he was visiting Sadie while Nancy was grieving the loss of her first husband. "The timing was just perfect."

By its nature, with proper care and nurture, as the years pass love blossoms like a flower in July. My wife and I married on August 12, 1967. With each passing anniversary, we revel in the security of our faithful, enduring partnership. The underlying feeling is that our mate will be there for us, no matter what happens. We accept each other's foibles, imperfections, and habits. That kind of acceptance produces an inner confidence that makes the days shine brighter.

You might not think so after reading this far, but Kathy and I are not that gooey-eyed and sentimental. We have never used the phrase "soul mate" to describe our match. We are simply sweet, loving, and committed to each other. Despite our all-too-human shortcomings, we believe our children have benefited from seeing good role models; they know what a good marriage looks like.

Because our marriage has endured, each of us knows the joy of getting to know another intimately—and to be known by that person. We have learned one of the secrets to a lasting relationship. I call it the "three Cs," which stands for "Communicate, Communicate, Communicate."

We met at the radio station where I first worked after college and married two years later. Her main role was always as my chief cheerleader. A self-described homebody, she is very close to our two children and has now taken on the role of doting grandma.

Still, encouragement is a two-way street. When we married, she had only a two-year associate's degree from college. In the 1990s, Kathy sensed that her time had come. Determined to complete her studies, she reenrolled in school. To support her, I took over many of the household management duties so she could complete her degree in psychology. She went on to teach adult literacy classes at a community college.

EMPOWERED BY LOVE

For both of us, love empowered us to go further than we could have individually. In a day when marriages seem to be crumbling at an increasing rate, it is easy to devalue the ideal of love. It is also often taken for granted, as if it were just there every day, like sunshine in the summer and cold in the winter. However, the power of love cannot be underestimated. I know because for the past two decades I have watched it transform lives and rescue children who otherwise would likely have wound up on society's scrap heap. These results prove love is more than a cliché.

Take Jacob, who was still a toddler when his mother left the family to return to her native country. He lived with his grandparents until he was twelve, then moved to a new city to live with his father and stepmother. There he fell in with the wrong crowd, joining a gang, getting involved in drugs, and receiving a criminal charge of auto theft. After running away from home multiple times, he wound up in one of our facilities.

While the temptation is to write off this kind of young man as hopeless, he showed otherwise. Touched by the love of Betty and Will, his caring houseparents, he went on to graduate from high school and enlist in the Marines. After the terrorist attacks of September 11, 2001, he sent a letter to Betty and Will from overseas, telling them he was getting ready to ship out at a moment's notice.

"Tell everybody that I love them and miss them tremendously," he wrote. "I want to thank you for all the things you have done for me. If it weren't for the two of you and the rest of the staff, I probably would not be writing you this letter. I just want to say thank you and I love you guys.... With the help of God, you all saved my life. Now it is my turn to help God save others."

Jason is another young man serving our nation in the Air Force, after graduating from The Citadel. He earned numerous awards at that famed institution, making the commandant's list three times, being named "Outstanding Air Force Cadet," and earning recognition as a superior performer in his Air Force training. As company commander during his senior year, he oversaw 104 cadets.

When he came to us, though, his life had been a disaster. After his father died when he was five, his mother started abusing drugs and alcohol, and him. He bounced around foster homes for eight years. But at one of our residential homes, he found the family he never had, recalling, "I'd wake up and know someone was there, that I'd have breakfast and go to school, that there'd be someone waiting for me when I got home."

With his basic needs met, Jason blossomed. He excelled at school, demonstrated leadership skills in the Reserve Officer Training Corps, and served on his home's governing council for five years. Propelled by love, he dreamed of a better future, saying, "It's easy to say I've been an abused child and act like a victim all my life. You can do that or you can say, 'I'm gonna stand up and make something of myself.'"[1]

The effect of love lasts for years, as Teresa discovered after suffering the heartbreak of an abusive marriage that ended in divorce. She turned to our agency for help, wanting to enroll in college and leave a life of welfare and other negative experiences behind. Although she received student loans and some financial aid, it still was not enough to cover expenses.

Thanks to our assistance, she graduated from the university and then went on to earn her master's degree. Today she is an eighth-grade teacher. In a long letter recapping her experiences, she concluded that after seven years as a college student, she felt that she had officially entered adulthood and self-sufficiency. Since education is important to her, all those late nights writing papers and studying for exams were worth it, and she was grateful for the opportunity to challenge herself. With the conquering power of love, dreams really can come true.

Chapter 5

Step 5: Find Passionate Pursuits

Here it is! The checkered flag! The cheers of 60,000 auto-racing fans reach a crescendo. Victory is a blink away, so is a hefty championship check and a NASCAR trophy to adorn the mantel. A flock of reporters and TV cameras await your every word...a dream come true.

Over the past twenty-five years, Kyle Petty has embraced this electrifying sensation multiple times. But it does not compare to the experience he and wife, Pattie, had at a camp in Florida for children with the disfigurement of cranial facial disease. But instead of feeling too embarrassed or self-conscious to venture into the open, 140 kids romped, laughed, swam, and fished.

The joy of seeing smiles on little boys' faces and lights flashing in little girls' eyes convinced them that they needed to build a similar camp near Kyle's hometown of Randleman, North Carolina. Patterned after several built by actor Paul Newman, construction costs alone surpassed twenty million dollars. Having raised several million dollars for children's hospitals in their annual Charity Ride Across America and millions more from corporate racing sponsors, they did not shrink from the task.

Winning races and accolades provides a good living, although it represents more grueling work than many fans envision. Still, that is not what God put them here to do, says Pattie, founder of the new Victory Junction Gang Camp. Crediting her husband with setting the family's "giving" tone, she sees racing as a platform God gave them to accomplish greater tasks.

"I have trophies in places around the house, but they don't have nearly as much meaning as when the phone rings and someone from camp says, 'Guess what? We just sold a building; we're closer to building the camp,'" she said before it opened in June, 2004. "Or someone sends one hundred bucks with a note that says, 'I want this to go to make sure another kid gets to come to camp.' That's huge."

Plans call for hosting up to 125 children per week in the summer and family retreats from September to May. Campers will not pay for sessions or amenities such as T-shirts, shoes, socks, hats, and transportation. Among the thirteen disease groups represented among the children will be kidney, heart, and liver disease; diabetes; spina bifida; AIDS; and sickle-cell anemia.

The last, which most commonly strikes African-Americans and Hispanics, especially touches Pattie's heart. Although this genetic cell defect affects more than 21,000 Americans, she sees it attracting little attention. Among its consequences is a limit of three degrees in sudden variations of body temperature. Greater swings can cause painful attacks on the nervous system. She gets excited describing the joy of these sickle-cell sufferers, many of them teens, diving into a swimming pool for the first time.

"Our camp will provide a room off the pool (it's called the French Fry Room at Boggy Creek Camp in Florida) where they go in and get their temperature gradually brought back to the normal outside temperature. It's something you don't normally think about."

The Victory Junction Gang offers the Pettys another benefit: a way to honor their son, Adam, who died in a racing accident in the spring of 2000. From the fourth generation of Pettys to climb behind the wheel, nineteen-year-old Adam was a strong camp supporter. He liked the equal treatment children would receive and funds going to a worthy cause.

Nothing will replace Adam. Mrs. Petty speaks of the void in their lives, a pain that increases with time and is hard to grasp unless one has lost a child. Still, she sees good emerging from tragedy. In the aftermath of his grandson's death, Kyle's father (racing legend Richard Petty) became a whole-hearted supporter, donating land and spending countless hours developing it. Pattie Petty has seen a groundswell of support from fans across the nation, many motivated by memories of her son.

So, while she may be nursing a wounded heart, losing Adam will lead to others' gain. She recognizes, too, that watching a child suffer from chronic disease—which often leaves parents financially devastated—may in some ways be tougher than losing that child to death.

"I really believe Jesus puts things on people's hearts," Pattie says. "Within every person God puts something in your life, or something on your heart, that you're supposed to do. My mother used to say that if you don't do those things and you don't follow what God wants you to do, then you're squelching the Holy Spirit that works in you. For some reason, God put on our heart children with chronic illness, disease, disabilities, or who are less fortunate."

From the Heart

Passionate pursuits—some find them in fishing, camping, politics, or charitable causes such as Habitat for Humanity. I draw energy from writing and speaking, which allow me to communicate powerful ideas. I love encouraging people to do their best by putting away the past, ignoring old voices that insist they cannot succeed, and releasing the "inner child" that still finds joy in daily life and dreams of bigger days to come.

Taking time to persuade, motivate, inspire, and stir others to action adds another duty to my crowded schedule. Nevertheless, I love doing it, especially speaking. There is something powerful about being invited into the circle of an audience and feeling that you are "at one" with them. When speaker and audience move together toward a common goal, it is like striking flint against steel. Fire!

Take a recent encounter, where I removed my mask of propriety, related some personal struggles, and shared a point of identification. It turned into a freewheeling, humorous, emotional, and passionate exchange. At that moment in time, the group and I felt united. I could sense their identification, smiles, joy, and acceptance.

Passionate pursuits demand flexibility. I once gave the graduation address at our local high school. Two days before, a well-known student had committed suicide. Scrapping my prepared script about the joys of graduation, I dug deep to offer words of grace and hope. Students, parents, and faculty alike needed balm for their wounds.

The impact of such honesty is awesome. Through moments of shared silence and making direct eye contact, I believe—and want them to believe—that no matter what their condition in life, they can move forward. The same happens in one-on-one settings. To penetrate exterior defenses, soak up another person's joy and pain, and let them know that at least one person seeks to understand, brings me indescribable pleasure.

You never know where such pursuits will lead. While working with youth in 1970, I encouraged young people to give themselves to something they passionately believed in. Imagine my delight and gratification thirty years later, when a member of that group donated a kidney to a student she barely knew. Jane McDuffie Smith received nationwide media attention for this literal sharing of herself with another. When I read that Jane credited me as one of the major influences in her life, tears filled my eyes.

The reason such exchanges work is because they come from the heart, produce results, and are given freely. Likewise, whatever your pursuits outside the setting where you earn your income, the most rewarding come from those that include giving yourself away.

Rick Lunnon discovered that when he started helping people on the lowest rungs of the world's economic ladder. A real estate developer in suburban Denver, Colorado, over the years he has overseen a variety of residential and mixed-use developments. He knows the thrill of a seven-figure income from closing real estate deals.

Yet if you ask what brings lasting joy, he talks about a home he and others from his church are helping build in Thailand. Calling it a "boys home" does not tell the whole story. Eventually it will provide a refuge for 200 youngsters orphaned by the plague of AIDS and other calamities. Some will also escape the horrors of that nation's thriving prostitution trade. Long-term plans include providing vocational training and Bible classes.

When Lunnon and his wife first visited Thailand in November of 2001, he wanted to inspect the land and develop an appreciation for the project. He quickly discovered that the Akha people desperately needed his expertise. Such talents as knowing one's way around engineering, land plotting, site development, and tricky negotiations were invaluable. Involvement proved to be more than a matter of throwing dollars at a worthwhile effort. Time, talents, and prayers represent equally precious commodities.

"I feel energized, excited, and humbled," says Lunnon, who returned to Thailand eight months later to help build a basketball court and parking lot at the site. "You fall in love with the people. They're very hospitable and gentle. For six months after my wife and I came back, we dreamed about them every night. They live on the equivalent income of $200 a year, but they taught us about giving."

Lunnon finds other rewards in this passionate pursuit. The smiles and hearty welcomes in Thailand make him feel like a hero. He will never forget enlisting help with site planning from some engineers in Denver. A few sentences into his presentation, two of them burst into tears. The men already had investigated getting involved in such an endeavor. Their company responded by sending three of them to Thailand and paying their salaries while they were away.

Lunnon's message is simple: with unprecedented wealth, time, and talents among those fifty and older, it is wise to invest in things that will last for eternity. He says that helping those who are too poor or too young to help themselves is a cure for American "affluenza"—the mistake of thinking that significance can be measured by the size of one's investment accounts, cars, boats, planes, or leisure pursuits.

"When you understand God's command for laying up treasures in heaven, you feel the urgency in converting talents for God's use," he says. "This is the only thing that counts."

VOLUNTEERS

Changing the world does not necessarily mean building a multimillion-dollar camp, speaking to crowds, or helping an impoverished ethnic group. Our children's homes in North Carolina draw considerable contributions from senior adults who are often overlooked and unappreciated. Besides offering their time, talents, and wisdom, many of these volunteers include us in their estate plans.

Nor do they necessarily want acclaim. In the mid-1990s, Charlotte Beck of Lexington began helping with administrative tasks at our headquarters, plus repairs and maintenance at various facilities. One time her husband bought Bibles for a group of boys after he saw them admiring another resident's copy.

"You're not going to make a big splash in their lives, but it takes a lot of little things along the way," Mrs. Beck says. "We like being those people in the background."

Every year Mitzi Moore of Winston-Salem visits several homes to plant flowers, wash windows, twirl a paintbrush, and talk with residents. Once she helped raise $1,000 to purchase a telescope for the educational program at our boys' wilderness camp. On another occasion, she led a summer Bible school at a home for those with developmental disabilities. She feels passionate about our cause because of her belief that childhood sets a pattern for life.

"Joy is in giving; it's not in receiving," says this former educator. "We've found that out in our latter days. We receive a lot of love from the children in return. When you give and don't expect anything in return, you feel really free. You're not bound by any restrictions or expectations."

For Stella Smith, interacting with residents substitutes for the warmth from the children she never had. Despite a long-time marriage, she never knew the joy of holding a baby until she visited our daycare nursery. "That broke the barrier between babies and me," says the Kings Mountain resident. "I loved babies, but before this I wouldn't touch them. They weren't mine."

She has touched older children, too, counseling disillusioned teens or offering comfort to those who have come from dysfunctional backgrounds—homes where alcohol has caused untold damage, siblings are in prison, or the child knew the horror of finding a parent dead from a drug overdose.

"I am trying to help them all I can," she adds. "I'm in touch constantly. If you have any concern for children at all, it tears your heart out. I keep going because I feel I can help."

Despite encountering horror stories, these caring seniors also hear about happy endings that represent dividends on investments of time, love, and effort. Retired teacher Jacque Burgess describes our homes as a "place of miracles" because of the positive impact they have on so many young people.

"It's amazing what happens in their lives," Burgess says. "You can talk about life-changing experiences. It turns them around from hopelessness to hope."

Playing that kind of role in another person's life will make you passionate, too.

Chapter 6

Step 6: Remember Nature's Nurture

A TOTAL ECLIPSE OF the sun. A once-in-a-lifetime experience. And I almost missed it.

Though more than thirty years have passed, this scene has etched itself into my mind. I remember vividly the rural roadside where I watched it, the awe that filled my spirit, and the overwhelming sense that I had witnessed a miracle only God could create.

Then in my last year of graduate school, news media in Raleigh, North Carolina, had informed readers that they would see a 97 percent eclipse. But one county south, the chances moved closer to 100 percent. At noon, two neighbors, my wife, and I spontaneously jumped into our car and drove off to witness this breathtaking event. We pulled off a lightly-traveled highway in front of an old cemetery, just minutes before it began.

I was not prepared for such awesomeness. Before we left Raleigh, a friend commented to me, "We'll just stay here and see 97 percent. Why do I want to drive an hour away? It's going to be virtually a total one here."

How sadly mistaken he was. Three percent of the sun still emits considerable light, as people assured us when we returned. The twilight that fell over the city and the darkness that enveloped us can be compared to the difference between seeing a picture of a million dollars and touching the cash with your hands. I can see why affluent people spend small fortunes flying to Argentina, Africa, or other exotic locales to witness a solar eclipse. It is that impressive.

As the late-winter sun faded to a shadow, we chuckled because the cows grazing in nearby fields turned around and headed for the barn. Slowly the sun's heat cooled as the moon passed between our planet and its source of warmth. Mesmerized by the black orb suspended in the sky, flickers of light dancing on its edges, we couldn't speak. I felt like a limited, finite, diminutive human being stepping into the presence of majesty. The thought struck me: "I'm seeing an awesome act of nature that I will probably never have a chance to see again."

Although the event lasted only about five minutes, we lingered for a half-hour as the afternoon sunlight reemerged. We did not want to leave what, for us, had become hallowed ground. On our return trip, the decision was unanimous: "We will never regret that we decided to come see this. We'll be able to tell people about it, but unless they experience it they'll never quite understand."

Years later, whenever I passed this spot on trips around the state, I would stop just to get out and gaze into the distance, my memories keeping the event alive. Each time, I felt renewed and refreshed, basking in the nurture of nature.

In today's television-computer-Palm-Pilot-cell-phone-addicted world, we face the danger of skipping such sights, thinking we can watch them on the evening news. That would be like receiving an invitation with five other people to a private meeting with the president of the United States and shrugging, "I don't think I'll go. I'm sure it will be on the news tonight. I'll just watch the other five sitting there in the Oval Office." When such opportunities arise, seize them. They may be just an hour away.

UNUSUAL ENCOUNTERS

Seeing the eclipse was my most magnificent encounter with nature, but not the only memorable experience. Several years before, I stepped out the door to drive to the radio station where I was working—and was greeted by a meteor shower. Known as the Leonid shower, a similar event in 2001 received constant media attention. But the event thirty-five years earlier was more spectacular, appearing like a Fourth of July fireworks display in the middle of November. Imagine 140 shooting stars per second—a rate of 500,000 per hour!

As with the sun's eclipse, I stood and marveled over the early-morning light show. Almost everyone has seen a shooting star. But this looked like an army of light-filled batons flashing across the horizon. Everywhere I turned I saw them rippling by, with the element of surprise adding to my delight. On and on it went for at least thirty minutes, filling me with wonder.

Unfortunately, cloudy weather prevented me from witnessing a repeat performance a few years ago. But my executive assistant had a similar reaction when she stepped out the door at 4:30 a.m. on a chilly November morning. Jennie told me later that it seemed as though time stood still: "It was as if I was part of something that I couldn't make, was bigger than me, and older than me. The word 'awesome' keeps coming back. There's a renewal in this. It makes you feel that everything is all right in the world."

More than a decade after I saw the sun disappear, I stayed up past 2 a.m. for an eclipse of the moon. Watching the earth's shadow cast upon the moon does not compare in grandeur to the sun's vanishing, but this event still carries a special memory. Shaking my eleven-year-old daughter awake, I rushed her outside, telling her, "I want you to see a total eclipse of the moon." "Tell me what it's about," she said as her eyes widened.

Lacking a science background, I stuttered my way through an explanation, but my lack of expertise did not bother her. Throughout the twenty-minute experience, her main question was, "Will the moon come back out again?"

"Probably," I replied with a smile.

More than twenty years later, she still remembers strolling outside as her mother and brother slept. Not only is this image burned in my mind, I am grateful I took the time to watch it with her. Since then, every time a lunar eclipse has made the news, cloudy weather has prevented me from seeing it again.

Nature has an awesome power, as noted by writer and teacher John Killinger. He talks of how the basic elements of earth, air, fire, and water instinctively draw him to God: "My own predilection is for water. When I was a boy, I could sit for hours staring at the surface of a small pond on my father's property or watching the stones and leaves and crayfish tracks beneath the clear water of a little stream. After I became a Christian, my praying often centered on these objects. There was no pantheism involved. I simply felt surrounded by the glory of God in his creation."[1]

WILDERNESS LESSONS

Most of my days are spent sitting behind a desk, talking on the phone, driving a car, making speeches, or calling on donors. But it was not just a change of pace that lured me to an outdoor center in the mountains to take part in a leadership training program. I hoped to learn to confront my fears, try new things, and build teamwork by hiking, climbing, rappelling down cliffs, and battling whitewater rapids.

I prepared for this grueling exercise with two months of training that included walking, bike riding, and a low-fat diet. Still, I approached this session nervously, particularly the solo rafting trip. While I had paddled a canoe as a boy expertly, I did not know a ducky (an inflatable kayak) from an igloo. Still, that day I bravely climbed into the water and later emerged with several valuable lessons:

- A good beginning is pleasant, but a bad beginning sharpens your resolve.

  I fell out of my ducky only once—as soon as I climbed into it. Though wet and embarrassed, I laughed it off and climbed back in. Now I knew what to do to keep from tipping over again. Most importantly, I saw that a rocky start can build integrity, character, and fortitude.

- Enjoy the view, but do not forget that a boulder may lie around the corner.

  We maneuvered down the Nantahala River. Like leadership and planning, the colorfully-nicknamed Nanny required a long-range view. Just when I thought I had conquered it, a huge rock appeared out of nowhere. I not only hit it, I wound up climbing on top of it. That forced me to learn my next lesson.

- Asking for help is wise.

  When you are lost or confused, do not insist on going it alone. And do not try to appear as though you are still in command of the situation. I successfully got relaunched after a buddy paddled over to pry me off the rock. But in my eagerness not to look helpless, I smacked him in the mouth with my paddle.

- Crossing the finish line is great, but do not relax until you make it.

  Even the final hundred yards of our eight-mile trip were not smooth sailing. Though we had survived the final rapid, several members of our entourage started coasting and wound up in the water. Until you complete a task, unforeseen obstacles may toss you for a loop.

While I did not set out to prove anything, in reality I felt I gained two new insights:

1. F-E-A-R is nothing more than False Evidence Appearing Real. Thus, we are not to Forget Everything And Run.
2. The greatest limitations we face are those we impose upon ourselves.

I have seen nature's educational value in other ways, particularly at the boys' camp that our network of children's homes operates. Up to fifty boys, ages eight to sixteen, reside there. Their education comes in a variety of settings, from planning outdoor trips, to drawing up menus, to setting a budget. Then there is the motivation of learning to finish tasks on a cold evening so they can climb into a warm sleeping bag.

The power of nature also unlocks deeply masked feelings. Several years ago one youth chose the quiet setting of a canoe to confide in his counselor how he felt about the horror of sexual abuse inflicted by his stepfather. Later, he said that was the best day of his life. Freed from this awful secret, he later transferred to a home closer to his native environs and formed a close relationship with his houseparents. A football player in high school, he graduated and is now making his mark in the world.

"That boy said he didn't know why, in the middle of that experience on the lake, that he felt able to talk to the counselor," says camp director Paul Daley, who related this story. "I think it was a combination of factors. The outdoors stimulates relationship-building. The nonthreatening setting was a key."

During his three decades of work with troubled youngsters, much of it in natural settings, Daley has seen a wealth of success stories. One that stands out involved a seven-week rafting trip down the Mississippi River from Cairo, Illinois, to New Orleans, Louisiana. One day on the trip, taken in the midst of America's bicentennial celebration, they saw President Gerald Ford cruising by on a paddleboat.

But it was not that glimpse that proved memorable. It was the fifteen-year-old who once wore two-foot-long, bleached blond hair and rarely bathed. His lack of cleanliness mirrored the anger he felt over abuse and broken family relationships. But floating down the Mississippi, he opened up. Nature changed his countenance so dramatically that when they returned and saw a slide presentation of their trip, even this youth did not recognize himself.

"Sometimes you forget where you started," Paul says with a smile.

SOLITUDE

One of the most meaningful experiences of my life came on a three-day silent retreat. All we did for seventy-two hours was eat, sleep, and reflect. Out of that sojourn came a little song I titled "My Secret Place." It goes simply:

MY SECRET PLACE

My Secret Place
To seek Your face
I know You there
I see You there

My Secret Place
Filled with Your grace
I feel You there
I touch You there

I know You best
When I can rest
At Your sweet side so dear
So come now, Lord
I want You, Lord
To be so close and near.

The inspiration for this tune came during walks in the woods. Being in nature and enjoying the solitude of a forest or a quiet lake gives me strength for the journey. Resting in nature draws me closer to God. I worship the Creator as I enjoy His creation. Best of all, you do not have to travel to the Grand Canyon or national parks such as Yosemite or Yellowstone. You can find that quiet place in a local park, or maybe even your backyard.

The danger in today's electronics-addicted world is forgetting to step outside. People can get so attuned to the Internet and computerized gizmos that they rarely emerge from their high-tech dungeons. Better to be like one of my staff members, who between appointments escapes from office pressures by sticking on waders and going fishing in the mountains. He comes back renewed and refreshed. That is the treasure nature offers each of us.

Chapter 7

Step 7: Seek Uplifting People

I BELIEVE HISTORY WILL judge evangelist Billy Graham as one of the most influential people of the twentieth century, not to mention one of the most admired. After first meeting him in 1967 at his boyhood home in Charlotte, North Carolina, I can see why. His enthusiasm inspired me like few men I have met. When he locked his penetrating blue eyes on me, I felt like I was the only other person in the room. The Scripture he quoted (Philippians 1:6: "Being confident of this, that he who began a good work in you will carry it on to completion until the day of Christ Jesus") helped resolve questions about my future during a period of soul searching.

I felt so inspired by his commanding presence that six months later I drove to his mountain home in western North Carolina, hoping to see him again. Instead, I met his wife, Ruth, who proved every bit as gracious and hospitable as her husband. Ironically, the Grahams had moved there to escape curiosity seekers. Yet she remained unflappable when my fiancée and I appeared in her driveway. She invited us in, made tea for us, and gave us an impromptu tour of their log cabin as their son, Ned, munched on a bowl of cereal.

We saw numerous pictures of Graham, his family, and some world-renowned figures. My favorite stop was at his private study, the place where he read, prayed, conversed with important figures, and made decisions. Not only did I marvel at the breathtaking view, but also over the unpretentious surroundings for a man then coming into his prime as an international figure and counselor to presidents and heads of state.

Seeking uplifting people is worth the time and effort it takes. Sure, they are fallible and prone to faults, mistakes, shortcomings, and the weaknesses that every single person possesses. But if you train your eyes on their talents and abilities, you will see something special that will lift your own aspirations. In Graham's case, here was a man who had fully yielded himself to God. Though an imperfect vessel, he told God, "Do with me whatever it is You have planned."

Such glimpses of greatness help move me beyond my limitations and help me appreciate the sacrifices such people make of their time, privacy, family life, and other simple pleasures so that society will benefit. Looking back, I cannot even say that my theological views meshed perfectly with Graham's, but that does not matter. I admire him, and the criticism he faced at various times through the years does not concern me.

I have met other uplifting people, some famous (such as President John F. Kennedy) and others who generally are not known outside my home state, except in certain professional circles. In every instance, I have taken away some insight, gem of wisdom, or personal observance about the way such folks handle themselves.

I will never forget meeting JFK as a college sophomore. Thanks to North Carolina Governor Terry Sanford's support of his candidacy, he visited the University of North Carolina's campus for "University Day" nine months after taking office. As a staffer at a local radio station, I secured a press pass and a seat on the front row. In addition to President Kennedy and Governor Sanford, another of my heroes sat on the podium: University President Bill Friday.

Since Kennedy was assassinated before I graduated, this turned out to be my only chance to see him in person, shake his hand, and listen to one of his speeches. Perhaps because of its uniqueness, this lives on in my memory as an electrifying experience. For a generation that came of age in the 1950s, the Massachusetts native brought a new dynamism and energy to the nation.

While it was a thrill to see a U.S. president up close, as the years passed I got to know the university's president much better. Not only did Friday and I grow up in towns ten miles apart, we shared some of the same values. His most impressive accomplishment during thirty years in office was consolidating sixteen independent state colleges into one cohesive system. He was so smart and powerful that when one governor wanted to meet with him, he drove to Chapel Hill instead of asking Friday to visit the Statehouse.

Politically savvy, Bill is a living example of maintaining calm under fire, how to graciously meet people, work with the news media, and be measured in one's thinking. He also took courageous stands when necessary. At a time when the Dixie Classic was one of North Carolina's most famous basketball tournaments, he canceled it after a taint of scandal surrounded the event. Though facing intense public criticism for the decision, he never backed down.

ENTHUSIASM-PLUS

When speaking to younger people, I counsel them to never consider anyone they meet insignificant, because all encounters have the potential for positive future results. They never know who is sitting next to them who may become the next great writer, educator, inventor, musician, or TV personality. In addition, seeking uplifting people does not solely mean chasing the rich and famous to ask for an autograph or a minute of their time. Remember the teacher, coach, Bible scholar, or craftsman who lives down the street.

In the spring of 2002 I returned to my hometown to look up ninety-five-year-old Love Dixon, the pastor who baptized me when I was eight. We spent two hours together comparing notes, reminiscing, and stroking each other's ego. Five days later, he had a heart attack. Because of that, I learned that if I want to meet with someone, I better not procrastinate. I could wake up one day and learn they are gone. Or, in Love's case, have to leave home to live with a daughter, ill health no longer allowing the luxury of a leisurely, extended conversation.

Lifelong encounters with uplifting people have shown me that enthusiasm is contagious and that expectations, attitude, and enthusiasm go hand in hand. Such positive personalities push us to do more, achieve more, and reach our full potential.

I love the story told by Millard Fuller, founder of Habitat for Humanity, in his book *The Theology of the Hammer*. Though now world-famous, in 1992 Habitat was still establishing itself. At the rate it was then building, he realized it would take 100 years just to replace the shacks in the region around Americus, Georgia. Thus, he presented a goal to his board to eliminate substandard housing in the members' county by the end of the decade. When the board went to table the motion, he stood on the table, ran a lap around the room, leapt over the table, and fell to his knees to plead with them to pass the initiative. Fuller wrote, "It worked! The board not only voted to proceed—the vote was unanimous!"[1]

That is the kind of impact uplifting people can make. Nor do they have to be as demonstrative as Fuller. Quiet enthusiasm does not need a "hip, hip, hooray" element to instill confidence. Nor are the people who uplift, direct, and guide us only in powerful positions. I have supervised some uplifting people whose giving of themselves has turned around thousands of young lives. Their work gives me hope that we can offer a better life to boys and girls scarred by hideous abuse and deprivation.

I have previously mentioned our boys' wilderness camp. I do not mean to single it out for praise, but there are many sparkling examples of that staff's excellence. At one statewide meeting, residents displayed crafts they had made, shared fishing stories, and moved many supporters to tears. A boy about ten years old took the microphone to thank everyone for praying for them, concluding, "One thing I've determined to do while I'm at camp is to be all that God intended for me to be."

That kind of statement originates with an enthusiastic, committed staff. These are the kind of dedicated, uplifting people who will take time away from their families to lead these boys on a three-week fishing, rafting, or camping trip. If that sounds easy, try doing it some time. But when a young boy says, "I don't feel dumped on; I feel like I'm a child of God," it makes the volunteers know that their sacrifices are worthwhile. I am grateful to know such positive examples of humanity's goodness.

BURNING BRIDGES

Just as you should seek uplifting people, sometimes you may need to avoid others who are critical, judgmental, or simply do not like you. I have lived long enough to know that none of us can please everyone. It matters not how strong your faith, solid your integrity, or gracious your character is. This truth reminds me of an ancient poem penned by a man who had a conflict with the Bishop of Oxford in England:

> I do not like thee, Dr. Fell
> The reason why I cannot tell
> But this I know, I know full well,
> I do not like thee, Dr. Fell.[2]

Generally, I counsel people to avoid burning bridges. Time has a way of healing wounds and settling differences that may not seem as important a few years after the fact. Yet, people who constantly belittle you, use you, or stab you in the back can be harmful to your mental health.

So are those who ignore you. Ever have an old friend who never bothers to answer e-mail, return phone calls, or otherwise keep in touch? I have, despite a closeness during our school days that I thought would endure for the ages. But this man has never lifted a finger to contact anyone in the "old gang." Over time, I realized he primarily wanted to use people. Were he to call today, I would be cordial, but doubt that I would go to the trouble of investing myself in a relationship.

Sometimes, the unpleasantness is more direct, such as a confrontation I had years ago with a woman who disagreed with one of my policy decisions. She accosted me after a meeting, the fire burning in her eyes so fiercely I assumed that if she had a weapon she might have attacked me. Ever dealt with someone like that? Not only are such incidents likely to spark anxiety, unhealthy eating habits, or depression, they usually upset you more than your detractor.

After another meeting where she again looked at me in red-hot fury, I thought, "Why am I letting her have such power over me? I need to forget her and move on." In such cases, I think the biblical admonition Christ gave his disciples when sending them out to talk with others applies: "If anyone will not welcome you or listen to your words, shake the dust off your feet when you leave that home or town" (Matt. 10:14).

ACCENTUATING THE POSITIVE

Ty Boyd is one of those uplifting people who inspired me to reach for the stars. A member of the North Carolina Broadcasters Hall of Fame, he later served as president of the National Speakers Association and has written several books. After an outstanding broadcasting career, he started his own communications organization. Executive Learning Systems has trained corporate executives, Olympians, and public speakers from thirty nations to put their best foot forward.

Earlier I mentioned working at a Chapel Hill radio station.

Ty hired me and showed me more than the ropes of broadcasting. Through his example, I saw that enthusiasm, a caring attitude, and concern for others will never grow old. He credits his parents with setting that standard, recalling how they always made him and his two brothers feel like stars. Later, he sought out teachers whose outlook always made him feel like he could do better.

"When you deal with positive people, it fuels your own perception of your value," he told me recently. "If other people see you in a negative light and you see yourself that way, you're not going to be successful. If you see yourself in a positive light, the feedback of positive people can help you achieve greatness. It's hard enough to break through in life. When positive people reflect back to you, it ignites your passion."

Businessman Nido Qubein, whom I will talk more about in the next chapter, credits his mother with first teaching him the value of associating with uplifting people. Just to show you that wise mentors do not need a PhD or an armload of awards, she had only a fourth-grade education. But she taught him a lifetime's worth of wisdom.

"She used to say to me, 'Nido, if you want to be a great person, you must first walk hand in hand and side by side with people who are great.' The point of her principle about walking alongside great people was that who you spend time with, you become."

In other words, if you want your vision for the future raised, seek out those who can do the lifting.

Chapter 8

Step 8: Do Good Deeds

NIDO QUBEIN IS a successful businessman who oversees a consulting company, the world's largest whole-wheat baking firm, and a thriving public speaking business, and is president of High Point University in High Point, North Carolina. But when he came to America with fifty dollars in his pocket, he did not know a word of English. Still, his goal of getting a college education and becoming something in this land of opportunity was the only motivation he needed.

He worked hard to pay for his tuition—ten hours a day after classes. As his second year neared an end, the president came to see him. Although Nido thought he was working for his education, he learned there was a significant gap between what he paid and the actual cost. The difference had been paid by a doctor in a nearby town.

"I'd love to meet this person and thank him or her for their kindness and generosity of spirit," the wide-eyed young man said.

"That's what makes this story so extraordinary," the president replied. "This doctor wishes to remain anonymous."

Returning home, Nido knelt by his bed and cried like a baby. That day, he vowed to God that as soon as he was working, he would establish a fund to help other young people attend college. He kept his promise. Over the past three decades the

Qubein Foundation has given away more than two million dollars in scholarships.

But this was not the only good deed that touched this Lebanese immigrant. For his final two years of undergraduate studies, he planned to transfer to another school. That meant he would need a car, but the $375 he had saved would pay only half the cost of a secondhand vehicle. One day he told the woman who managed the rooming house where he lived. He shrugged that it was not a big deal, it just meant he would have to save another $375.

"At the end of the month I got my bank statement, and I had $750," Nido recalls. "I remember thinking, 'I love this country. The bankers don't know how to add.' Then I thought, 'Did she do this? This woman who's making $100 a month from Social Security and $100 from the college?' I went to see her, and she said, 'I decided I would rather park my money in the life of a budding young man than in my savings account.'"

How much value did these good deeds, done largely in secret, add to our society? Count the earnings power and increased self-esteem of those scholarship recipients, the vast number of employees at Qubein's multiple enterprises, those whose lives have been enriched by his companies' products and services and—you would probably run out of digits on your calculator.

THE POWER OF GOODNESS

No matter how modest or significant, such selfless gestures show that the greatest investments we make are not in the stock market but in other people. Good deeds have a lasting quality that often outlives us, touching, inspiring, and exhorting others to similar action, thus making the world a better place to live.

My first glimpse of their power came as a second-grader. Our elementary school principal, Robert K. Hancock, served as leader, historian, motivator, mathematician, and musician. Living beside the school, it became an extension of his immaculate personality. More important, he believed in strengthening the intellect and saw that his students received a first-rate education.

You may have been touched similarly by a teacher, coach, tutor, or professional mentor. Still, there is something that makes folks such as R. K. Hancock stand out from the crowd. He treated his position like a calling, not just a job. Because of that, he felt motivated to do a good deed that resolved what could have been a monumental personal embarrassment.

In our modest, small-town building, the school had converted a large classroom into a cafeteria. But sparse seating meant our class ate lunch at our desks. This day, I drew the assignment of returning plates to the cafeteria, which meant a trip down a long flight of stairs. On the fifth step from the bottom, my foot slipped. Plates and food sailed into orbit.

When I looked up, Mr. Hancock hovered over me. Silently, he brushed me off, helped me gather up the dishes, and made sure I was all right. No scolding, no criticism, no lamenting over my mess, no embarrassing questions. He just showed me compassion and concern. That day I learned a valuable lesson about extending a helping hand.

Because of his example, my parents' teaching, and the guidance of pastors, Sunday school teachers, and caring mentors, I came to embrace the value of good deeds. While I cannot draw a straight line connecting R. K. Hancock to an episode in my office decades later, a link still exists.

Several years ago, a single mother came to see me, frantic with concern. She was about to be evicted and lose her car. Like those plates I dropped as a boy, it looked as though she had simply made a mess of her life. But I understood the extenuating circumstances, starting with a deadbeat dad who refused to pay child support. Her parents could not offer any more help. Nor could she get a loan from her employer. Facing a 5 p.m. deadline, I represented her appeal of last resort.

Reaching into my desk, I gave her a $500 check. As a look of overwhelming gratitude covered her face, I said, "You better get down to the bank and take care of these bills right now."

That was risky. She could have vanished with my money. But she paid back the loan and got her life back on track. She will never forget my kindness, just as I will never forget helping her. Sure, there will always be freeloaders looking for a handout. But this woman had simply been dealt a bad hand. Helping her brought me no recognition, since she would never want to be identified as the recipient. But personal warmth and satisfaction always outlive applause.

9-11-01

This date will forever symbolize one of America's darkest moments, when thousands died at the hands of terrorists. Yet, triumph emerged from tragedy. In our darkest hour, good deeds shone as rays of comfort, hope, and encouragement to millions devastated by the loss of friends and family, or who were numbed by this vicious attack on our nation.

Countless stories have been told about the kindness demonstrated by volunteers who came to New York and Washington, D.C., from every walk of life. Yet, it is worth sharing a couple of examples of the tenderness and care that illuminated the spirits of so many.

Insurance agency owner Charles Fox and his wife, Patricia, were among twenty volunteers from my state who traveled to Washington, D.C., less than twenty-four hours after an airliner crashed into the Pentagon. Soon they were handing water, cookies, and other refreshments to firefighters, relief workers, and Pentagon staffers trying to restore order amid chaos.

Patricia still feels humbled by the experience of seeing this devastation, yet also basking in the glow of the appreciation expressed to their team. She loved watching strangers come together in a unified purpose. "We were just providing a meal and letting them know we cared, that we loved them and God loved them. We didn't preach that, we just tried to show it."

Offering help is a lifestyle for her husband. The Boone, North Carolina, resident has joined disaster relief missions since the late 1980s. Working without pay for days stretching from daylight past dark, he has aided victims of nearly a dozen tornadoes, floods, and hurricanes.

"It's hard to express what I feel," Charles says of these good deeds. "I feel like I'm doing what I'm supposed to be doing, what as Christians we all should be doing. The satisfaction of helping somebody is all I need."

This giving continued long after the dust settled—literally. Nearly two months after the attacks, Andy Abbott of Apex, North Carolina, and six other people drove to Ground Zero to help clean nearby apartments that were still caked with dust. At one building, volunteer crews had earlier removed six inches of caked debris, but another inch had resettled in its place.

It was not just the cleaning, vacuuming, and packing assistance the people valued, but the volunteers' presence.

Andy remembers one woman who lived two blocks from the World Trade Center, far enough away that she did not qualify for the municipal assistance that went to those in the immediate vicinity. Even more unsettling was her shattered sense of security.

"She needed the cleaning, but she needed someone to be with her," says Abbott, a manager at a manufacturing plant. "Eight weeks later there was still a nervousness about her. Just being there and showing her people cared meant a lot. There was a woman in another complex who also needed someone to come in, clean up, and talk to her. I think showing those two ladies Christian love was more important than any cleaning we did."

ROUSING RELATIONSHIPS

Our children's homes are centers of good deeds. Thousands of people give freely of their financial resources to sustain our work. Volunteers help fix up our facilities and spend time with residents, brightening their lives. Childcare workers and social workers give far more of themselves than required by standard job descriptions, becoming surrogate parents and beacons of light to those who have been abused and misused.

Yet, this ethic of good deeds spread further several years ago through an initiative that revitalized our network into a more cohesive unit. For weeks I struggled to name this effort. Then, suddenly I awoke in the middle of the night, with initials flashing through my mind: QSTQR. I accepted this inspiration as a divine gift, since it took several days to determine all the words for this acronym: "Quality Service Through Quality Relationships."

Since management gurus have devised similar slogans, this may not sound that revolutionary. But from this fertile soil sprang a new element of caring. Employees went out of their way to become a team. Camaraderie from monthly luncheons and periodic weekend outings turned into gestures such as sending cards or visiting others in the aftermath of sickness or a death in the family.

Stepping out of my presidential garb, one day I joined other management personnel to serve lunch to secretaries. One of my longtime employees enjoyed purposely dropping her silverware and constantly asking me for more iced tea. But it underscored a significant idea, as I told one woman, "In this organization there's no such thing as anybody being 'just' an anything. You're as important a cog in this wheel as I am. I never want to hear you say, 'I'm just a secretary' again."

Nor did this giving stop at the office door. Determined to help the community, the director of the daycare center on our main campus started monthly parenting seminars and support groups. Children in an after-school program learned sign language to various songs and visited churches, rest homes, and civic events to perform. They also created birthday cards and baked cakes for children at the home.

The most innovative outreach? A new "fatherhood initiative" to encourage more fathers, stepfathers, and grandfathers to get involved with their children. That may sound ordinary, until you consider that 30 percent of the kids in our county do not have a daddy at home. Similar figures exist nationwide.

Thus, for the first time, men came to the center to read stories, join kiddies on the playground, and take trips to the zoo. One father who works as a telephone lineman wore his hobnail boots on a visit, climbed a pole, and ran a phone line to their room. His little boy, who previously had a hard time fitting in, became a class hero and made new friends.

By the second year of this program, more than 50 percent of preschoolers had a father figure more closely attuned to their lives. While social scientists would say that tangible results cannot be measured, we know from other studies that children lacking paternal involvement face an increased risk of poor grades, drug abuse, early pregnancy, and dropping out of school.

So, has it been worth it? Ask the little children who wear happier faces, looks of contentment, and pay closer attention in class. They will tell you that this good deed changed their lives. Freely extend a hand to help someone, and you may never be able to measure exactly what it did. Yet, look closely, and you will be able to see the results in that person's eyes.

Chapter 9

Step 9: Be a Mentor

S UNDAY MORNING AT dawn is a great time for sleeping. At this moment, I could only wish I were back in bed. It was my freshman year in college and the first day of work at the local radio station (this was before the days of 24/7 broadcasting.)

I had just flicked the various switches to the "on" position to deliver the waking sounds of WCHL Radio to the community of Chapel Hill. Next I checked the meters and panels, finished the established routine, and waited. Nothing. I fiddled with a few switches, trying to amend the sequence. Still nothing. What was wrong?

You probably know the feelings of panic. Beads of sweat popped out on my forehead. My armpits felt damp. Air time was minutes away, and I could not get the power on!

Frantic, I called the program director who had hired me. From the moment I met Ty Boyd (one of those uplifting people I mentioned in chapter 7), I knew he was special. When he arrived after throwing on some clothes over his pajamas, he proved it with grace and humor. Boyd could have raked me over the coals, even fired me. Instead, he acted as though it was Friday afternoon. Turning the right switches, he quickly had the power humming. Smiling, he said, "That probably happened to me the first time I was on the air."

Those few minutes were worth more than a semester's

worth of lectures. From this incident I learned to be patient with others when they make mistakes, which has helped me in several leadership roles. Ty taught me many other valuable lessons, including the infectious value of enthusiasm. Though Chapel Hill is well known because of the University of North Carolina, it is not a major metropolis. But from this launching point Boyd became a statewide broadcasting legend. Eventually he moved to Charlotte, then into a second career as a presentation trainer and speaking coach. In this latter role, he has helped train me.

Ironically, although I had known Ty for decades, only recently did I learn about the two men who influenced him, one of my favorite mentors, to embark on a new career. One man he never met: Earl Nightingale, a Chicago-based commentator and sales executive who produced messages such as "Strangest Secret," in which he emphasized how we become the product of our thoughts. Every time Ty drove to a pageant or speaking appearance, he played (and replayed) Nightingale's recordings.

The other was Charlie Cullen, a salesman and humorist who traveled across the nation, speaking to sales reps, corporate employees, and other audiences. Ty will never forget the spark that persuaded him to leave broadcasting. After one of Boyd's speaking appearances, Cullen put an arm around him and said, "Ty, you can do what I do."

"It was like Joe DiMaggio putting his arm around a rookie," Ty recalls. "Those few words changed my life. He was saying, 'I play in the big leagues, and you can too.' Charlie made me feel so special. If you don't have mentors, someone in your corner, or an encourager in many aspects of life—parents, people in civic groups, and so on—life can be mighty tough."

THE VALUE OF MENTORS

The value of mentors rarely can be measured in specifics, yet over time we can see how much they mean to our lives. All of us need mentors to show us the ropes and provide inspiration. And, because of the fast-paced age in which we live, mentoring is increasingly important.

Famed speaker Zig Ziglar is a legend in sales and marketing. His enthusiastic reminder that you can get what you want in life by helping others get what they want has motivated countless people. It is easy to perceive that someone in the public eye has always been on top. But in his autobiography, the Dallas-based speaker and author reveals a string of missteps, impetuous moves, and mistakes that plagued him earlier in life.

Mentors helped turn him around. He mentions several, such as the supervisor who told him he could become his company's national sales champion. The man who first hired him reminded him that true joy comes from helping someone else achieve success. But most notable was Bernie Lofchick, the first person outside his immediate family who believed Ziglar had a future as a public speaker.

"Of all the things Bernie Lofchick has contributed to me and our relationship, the unflagging belief he has in me and the encouragement he has given me to continue my speaking and writing has been of utmost value," Ziglar writes. "Everyone needs a Bernie in his or her life. Without one, I suspect it is impossible to realize your full potential and to have the heart and stamina to stick with the ambitions of a lifetime."[1]

This is what Ty did for me. Not only did I admire him for his talent, he reached out to me and made me believe I could do great things. But he was not the only one. Just as many friends enrich our lives in various ways, it takes mentors from a variety of backgrounds to help us develop well-rounded skills.

In my case, three pastors who guided me from preschool through college were incredibly influential. From Love Dixon, my boyhood pastor I mentioned in chapter 7, I learned the art of loving pastoral skills. Wilburn Hendrix, who guided me through the rapidly-changing teenage years, taught me about public speaking. He also convinced me that God could use me in His service, although at the time I had my heart set on a career in broadcasting. Next came Hoyle Allred, who taught me the value of administration (and some days it seems like all I do is push papers around.)

Then there was Bill Friday, the former University of North Carolina president who became my hero. A gentle-spoken man, he grew up about ten miles from my hometown. This small-town boy overcame the strikes of a broken home, childhood poverty, and other obstacles to earn a law degree and become one of our state's most noted educators. Although a private person, he functioned in the most public of circumstances. Because of Friday, I learned the importance of self-awareness and focusing on my life's mission. He taught me that if I get too caught up in public recognition or looking for acclaim, I can easily lose my focus.

Bill also taught me grace under fire. One of the crowning achievements in my two decades at our children's homes was persuading him to join our board of trustees for a four-year term. He brought an incredible presence to our organization, especially when a newspaper unfairly attacked one of our homes and its staff. These critical articles appeared a week before a board meeting, touching off endless discussions about an appropriate response.

Then, with a few well-chosen sentences at the board meeting, Friday laid the matter to rest: "Don't try to take on a newspaper. You've done what you need to do with damage control, to reassure the staff, and let the kids know everything is going to be all right. Now just let it go." Those words were like pouring a soothing salve over troubled hearts. We weathered that storm with strength and resolve, responding to the crisis instead of hiding and licking our wounds.

Much of this crisis response can be credited to Friday's past teachings and those words of wisdom. He taught me that you have to make decisions, live with them, and move on.

PASSING IT ON

As one of Zig Ziglar's mentors told him, joy comes from watching others succeed. Just as others have helped guide our aspirations, as we grow older we need to hand off life's lessons to others. We should continually strive to make life better for coworkers, friends, family, and acquaintances. Making a positive impact on another person's life gives one a warm glow, a sense of purpose, and the kind of personal rewards that a paycheck and incentive bonuses will never match.

In chapter 5, I mentioned one of those I mentored, Jane McDuffie Smith, the teacher who donated one of her kidneys to a student. Two others I worked with during their college years went on to become ministers, one with a statewide denominational organization. We became close while I was overseeing a college coffeehouse for disenfranchised young people, those who grew up outside the comfortable confines of well-adjusted families and Sunday church services. For two years we attracted crowds of up to 200 every Friday and Saturday night, reaching those who otherwise were not likely to hear much "God talk."

Steve Sumerel has since become a counselor to families and those struggling with substance abuse. His outreach to society's downtrodden includes a summer retreat for people who have AIDS or are HIV positive. Although such respected figures as evangelist Franklin Graham have talked about extending help and comfort to such folks, in many quarters AIDS sufferers remain outcasts. When I spoke at a recent recognition dinner in his honor, the love and affection on the faces of those he has touched shone like spotlights.

Steve Jolly is now pastor of a church in Virginia, where he invests himself in people of all ages. For more than twenty years, he was an associate pastor, working primarily with youth. This articulate leader still provides a valuable guiding hand to young people, many who have grown up and call him a "blessing." I think of both of these Steves with the same kind of admiration I have for my own son.

Passing it on is something we can all do, especially those who have children (whether your natural offspring or step-children). Given the giants of peer pressure, omnipresent media, and unhealthy cultural influences, too many parents today underestimate the impact they make on their children's lives. No matter what circumstances you face, your gifts of time, guidance, and love will still go a long way.

Early on, I was a junior high and high school disk jockey. One of the reasons I was successful as one of the youngest in the nation at age fourteen was my father's tutoring. An insur-ance salesman and music leader at our church, Dad was not a radio expert. But he listened closely as I did mock broadcasts into a tape recorder and critiqued my performances. He would tell me things such as, "You need to say 'pro GRAM,' not 'pro GRUM,'" or "Don't pronounce the 'T' in often." Later, when I started developing my speaking abilities, he reminded me, "You need to talk to an audience like you're talking to the per-son on the back row."

Even if you are not a parent, or those years have long since passed, you can still be an encourager. My ten-point list on how to encourage others starts with the gifts of presence and listening. Being there when someone needs advice, feedback on an idea, a shoulder to cry on, or just to vent a little frustra-tion speaks volumes about caring. Listen with your heart as well as your head, sensing the underlying pain or motivation behind the words. The rest include:

- Be sensitive to the person's circumstances and the dynamics of events in his or her life. If you do not know what is happening currently, ask.

- Get to know the whole person, his or her personal-ity, likes and dislikes, and what is important to this individual. Wise fundraisers know that the secret to success is not walking into someone's office with a hand out, but first chatting about the pictures of their children or grandchildren on the desk or the fish mounted on the wall.

- Remember, you are there to make a difference in that person's life, not brag about your own accomplishments. It is always better to ask questions than to make declarations.

- Start with the premise that no matter what wrongs they have done, there is also the capacity for good in every person. Everyone can be encouraged to be their best. Remember, whether they live in a million-dollar home, a middle-class neighborhood, or a shanty on a creek bank, you can always find people hiding their pain behind a mask.

- No matter what their age, everyone needs a word of hope. You may be the one to lift their spirits.

- Do not try to overstretch your expertise to come up with sparkling words of wisdom. It is often the "little" things that make a difference.

- This one I learned from my father: a person's name is his or her most important possession. Use it often.

- Love yourself and love others.

The underlying philosophy behind this list is that everyone has a responsibility to fill others' cups. When you take time to be a mentor, you are passing on the kind of riches that will outlive you, extending your influence to generation after generation.

Chapter 10

Step 10: Give Yourself Away

ARLY IN HIS acting career, Robert DeNiro played what I consider to be one of his most powerful roles. In *The Mission,* he portrays Roderigo Mendoza, a mercenary working among the Indians of South America. A ruthless slave trader, he treats the Indians as if they have no souls or sensibilities. But his world plunges into chaos after he kills his brother in a dispute over a woman.

Mendoza struggles mightily with grief and remorse. Finally, a Jesuit friend, Father Gabriel, persuades him to atone by choosing his own penance. Thus, Mendoza winds up dragging his suit of armor and sword around by a rope attached to his waist. He does this for months, laboring through the jungle's mud, waters, and stifling humidity, and up the mountainsides. Once a rushing waterfall nearly sweeps him to his death.

When he recovers and maneuvers his way to safety, some Indians recognize him; he had captured and sold their sons and brothers during his slave-trading days. Seeing his penitent attitude, one of them cuts the rope holding his armor and sends it crashing down the rocks. He is free. Renewed, Mendoza devotes his energies to studying Christianity and building a mission church in the jungle interior. After a rotten beginning, his life turns around. The mission becomes his life.

Though many years have passed since I saw this film, it left lasting memories. Unfortunately, I did not save a newspaper story about it, where a reporter interviewed theater-goers about their reactions to the film. But I remember some of their comments. One man said it made him question his life and how selfish he had been. A woman said it made her think that we are placed on earth to do good. The most moving statement came from a middle-aged stockbroker, who said he would like to start over, with a real mission in life.

Back in the 1990s, a movement blossomed that encouraged people to write a personal mission statement. While that trend has passed, the underlying need is still fresh. Finding a driving purpose in life—one more meaningful than making it until Friday afternoon to collect a paycheck—gives you purpose, focus, and direction. A passion for living will make life more than a struggle for survival.

The fictional Mendoza found one of the secrets to a happy life: giving yourself away. This ethic runs 180 degrees opposite the materialism that infects America. Yet it is one of the secrets to a rich life that brings lasting rewards. I am not just refer-ring to good deeds, which I mentioned in chapter 8, though these may be linked. Giving yourself away can be a corner-stone of your occupation, a way to make your retirement years meaningful, or simply a habit incorporated into your lifestyle. I think of the woman I know who bakes bread constantly, just to give the loaves to neighbors, friends, and loved ones.

People who give freely of their time, talents, and energies make lasting impressions. One of the most dynamic professors I ever had in graduate school was a man who once lived on the campus of the Mills Home, which serves as both a children's home and the headquarters for our statewide organization. Marc Lovelace moved here as a high school freshman when his father became principal of the on-campus school. In a note he sent to me after we published a history of the organiza-tion, Lovelace said living here "gave me a warm and sensitive heart towards a segment of humanity that I had never known. There, I found an appreciation for a better life."

Years later, as a graduate student, I saw the long-term impression this experience made on him. A professor of archeology, Lovelace was one of the toughest professors I ever studied under, but also one of the best. A brilliant man, at his core was a desire to teach his students lessons that would last a lifetime. Giving of himself constantly, he literally made the Bible come to life. Lovelace would explain how Middle Eastern archeological digs had uncovered household gods and other objects mentioned in Old Testament books. To show you how strongly other students felt about him, today many of their sons bear the name of Marc (an unusual spelling.) My only regret was that after my first year, he moved to another university.

No Islands

So many people want to find themselves, when all it takes is giving themselves away. John Donne's famous quote, "No man is an island" still rings true. We weren't designed to live in isolation, but in community, where relationships enrich our lives and balance our outlooks. Giving ourselves away helps others and brings us intangible rewards. A former board member of our organization, Fleet Allen, used many of his retirement years to help elderly people complete income tax forms at no charge. I see other examples all around me:

- A secretary on our campus often says, "I think it's wonderful that they will pay me to do something I love so much." She is not just earning brownie points with the administration. Her actions show she means it.

- When my executive assistant was on vacation a couple years ago, she made an appointment for a facial. The woman who gave her the treatment asked, "Do you believe they pay me to do something that makes people feel so good?"

- It may sound like bragging, but our daughter, Julie, is an expert massage therapist. She is so gifted that once when I wanted to give a staff member a special birthday gift, I bought the person a massage. Sure, Julie has the training, but it goes beyond that. She gives her all to help people release tension and stress. As this staff member says, "You haven't lived until you've had a massage by Julie."

While I may earn a living directing a network of children's homes, if the only thing this job brought me were a salary, I would feel miserable. To see a staff member achieve personal and professional growth, or a once-sullen child stand tall with his head back, shoulders squared, and a smile on his face, is the kind of bonus I crave. Around here we like to say that we are "joy geologists." One of the most telling truths about my job is that after two decades, I still can wake up and smile as I say, "Thank God, it's Monday."

With 350 employees and serving 2,000 children at our facilities each year, this operation is definitely something much bigger than I am. Yet I have a part, even if it is a very small one, in making life special for each employee and child who comes our way. If I successfully direct my management group, then this empowerment can flow to the other staff members and on to the children and their families.

Granted, I often feel pressure. Not only are our staff and those we serve counting on me to make good decisions, so are our vast network of volunteers and financial supporters. There are challenges, such as meeting the budget and setting the corporate tone and direction. When push comes to shove, all eyes fall on me. The expressions on people's faces say, "Okay, we've done all we can do. Now what do you say? What's the word?"

Not that I am looking for sympathy. This is what I am paid to do, and I have to accept everything that comes with the job. That includes the wounds I feel when someone attacks me or another employee. Still, the rewards far outweigh the responsibilities and pressures. At times I am stressed and weary, but I am also humbled, gratified, inspired, and pleased that I have a mission to accomplish. I am grateful God has given me the energy and talent to be a part of something bigger.

THE GRAND PLAN

Many people struggle to find that passion, that cause to which they can commit their lives and joyfully give themselves away. There are no simple formulas, although a successful search starts with determination. As famed British Prime Minister Winston Churchill used to say, "Never give up." As a parallel, I would add, "Never fear failure." Too many timid souls never attempt to do anything because they are afraid of failing. But failure is both a learning opportunity and a way to move closer to your goal.

Accessing the grand plan for your life calls for sensitivity, openness to change, prayer, asking a lot of questions, and preparation. You also need the willingness to risk ridicule from others. If you decide to rise above the crowd and take a new direction in life, naysayers will be standing by to second-guess your motives. They will offer comments such as, "You shouldn't try that.... You'll never make it.... Who do you think you are?" Resist such negativity, for often it comes from those who regret missing their chance.

As one who is moving past what most would consider middle age, I can assure those who are younger that it is always better to look back on your life with fond memories of what you did instead of regrets over what you missed. It takes courage to step out of the box and change, which is why I advised earlier to surround yourself with uplifting people.

While stepping into the future, never allow yourself to get paralyzed by fear of the unknown or longing for the past. Your mind can play tricks on you and make you think the past was more wonderful than reality would show, if it were possible to beam it onto a large-screen television. Worst of all, continually yearning for the past is a sure way to miss opportunities to march into the future.

The children of Israel did this while they were headed for the Promised Land that God had promised to lead them to after they escaped 400 years of slavery in Egypt. For those who are not familiar with the biblical story, twelve spies went to scout out the land. Ten of them came back with a bad report: there were giants in the land, much too powerful for Israel to overcome. Only Joshua and Caleb insisted that they could meet the challenge.

Instead of listening to the promise of victory, the people embraced fear and discouragement. They wanted to choose captains to lead them back to Egypt, although it was a place of slavery under cruel taskmasters. Earlier, the first time they ran short on food in the desert, these grumblers—wearing the brightest of rose-colored glasses—mentioned only the wonderful food they enjoyed in the comfortable surroundings of Egypt. Unfortunately, that same spirit prevailed again. Missing their golden opportunity to enter the Promised Land, most of them died in the wilderness.

Likewise, we can miss opportunities today. How?

- By being afraid to move forward. Every time we contemplate change, giants (real or imagined) will challenge us. We can retreat to the comfort of a stale existence, but we are settling for a slavery of safety and boredom.

- By forgetting what the past was like. The pursuit of nostalgia affects every era. In recent years a "retro disco" craze erupted. When discos were hot in the 1970s, some were yearning for the 1950s. In the 1950s, others were recalling the good old days of the 1930s, when the Great Depression left many Americans unemployed and on the edge of starvation. What not-so-perfect past did you leave behind?

- By lacking the commitment to move forward.

We all want to enter the promised land of fulfillment, but we forget it carries a price of honesty, patience, kindness, giving, and faithfulness.

Opportunities pass people by every day. Instead of staying in troubled cities where their presence could make a pronounced difference, stable families, businesses, and churches migrate to the suburbs. Bright teens with college scholarships who could go on to great futures, thus helping others, instead skip class, flunk out, and wind up in minimum-wage jobs. Retirees with a wealth of experience and expertise waste their talents in idle pursuits of pleasure.

However, giving yourself away for something bigger than yourself calls for adopting a stance of readiness. Life is not a dress rehearsal; this is it. We are put here for a few brief moments, and if we do not take advantage, it will pass us by. The worst thing we can do is gaze over our yearbook of life and say, "Why? Oh, why?" when the person who wants to be part of something bigger is always looking ahead and saying, "Why not?"

Remember, when you start with the core value of giving yourself away, you will move on to become a blessing to others—and wind up happier yourself.

Chapter 11

Step 11: Receive Life

WHEN I REFLECT on the riches my parents left me, the treasures are not the monetary gifts they gave me growing up, nor the estates they left to me, their only son. Rather, it is the lasting inheritance they provided—qualities such as dignity, faith, their hard-working nature, and the enduring sense that honesty, effort, and integrity ultimately will triumph. I did nothing to deserve such caring, loving parents. They gave me the gift of life. All I had to do was receive it graciously.

I especially cherish the way my mother departed this earth just one day shy of what would have been her eighty-third birthday. Just hours earlier, as we drove to see her in western North Carolina, she gave the nurses a directive: "I want you to wash my hair and put on my makeup. I will then see Mickey (my longtime nickname) and will get ready to die tonight." They protested that the task would be painful for her, and difficult, because of overnight fluid build-up in her body. Guess who won the argument?

When we arrived after the three-hour drive, she could barely speak, but sat up in bed with silver hair shining. When I told her how beautiful she looked, she smiled. Calling my wife over to share a few words, she soon faded into unconsciousness. For several hours, I held Mom's hand, softly patting it and stroking her arm. Previously, we had shared our deepest feelings; now understanding ebbed and flowed between my fingers and her skin. Without a word, we celebrated, grieved, explained, and affirmed each other.

Suddenly, she removed her hand from my grasp. Later, I learned that is common for the dying. They want a private moment as they close life's door and prepare to walk through another. After a few minutes, she opened her eyes and beckoned me to come close. Whispering, "I love you," she closed her eyes. Those were her final words.

I have often thought that this would be a sterling legacy to leave my children: to pass away gently with them in my presence, letting them know I love them, and knowing that I will live on through them and successive generations. Like Mom, I want to leave with no regrets. Thanks to her example and others, I know that if we treat every moment as precious with those who matter to us, we will have few regrets.

On the other hand, if we do not graciously receive life as a gift, we may find it suddenly snatched away. Taking people for granted is a sure path to emotional poverty. To live a happy, fulfilling life, we need to fully explore, appreciate, and experience relationships with family, friends, and acquaintances. Because of the boundaries of time and human limitations, we cannot be close to vast numbers of people. But we can be willing receptacles to the value that others lend to our lives, no matter how small.

Receiving life means also receiving what comes after this earthly life. Because I believe in life after death, I do not accept the premise that our story ends when the funeral director lowers us into the ground. I live with the expectation that I will see my mother again, and that my children and grandchildren will one day see me again. Critics have either derided the idea or paid lip service to God's existence, but faith in God is the essence of my hope.

ENDURING TREASURES

No matter where in the world you live, people love their "stuff." Humans make an art of piling up furniture, jewelry, cars, countless trinkets, tools, and electronic gadgets, only to see it fade into meaningless piles of junk near life's end. I knew a man who filled not one but two houses with strange treasures. He would save old bottles and discarded car fenders "just in case." His collections stacked up to the windows, overflowed onto the porch, and sometimes spilled into the yard. Twelve years after his death, his old car was parked outside his country home, rusting into nothingness.

We get it backwards when we fantasize that things can bring us happiness. Friendships and intimate relationships represent true riches. I saw an amusing, yet poignant, illustration of this in one of my favorite comic strips, "For Better or Worse." In this episode, the main character's father is getting ready to move into an apartment to be closer to the widow he started dating after his wife died. The occupant who is departing shows him around, while mentioning that the problem with nursing homes is space: "I'll have a small room and a shared commode. This is what I'm taking. Mostly photographs, a favorite chair, a reading lamp...I won't miss the ornaments or the furniture."

At that point the widow responds, "But you have some real treasures here!" The woman replies, "People are my treasures now. These are just 'things.'"[1]

Malcolm Tolbert, a friend and former professor, pointed out that enough money to buy necessities is important, but beyond that we should not worry about material things. Before this comic strip appeared, he mentioned to me that what really matters is people—family, friends, and others who really care about you. "Relationships give depth to life and make life worth living," he says.

"I realized a long time ago that no matter how much you have, you can only wear one suit at a time, drive one automobile at a time, watch one TV at a time, and eat one meal at a time," he told me. "If you are able to do these things, you should be happy with what you have.

"We receive life one moment at a time and should not presume on the future. If we need to tell someone we love him or her, we should do it now. If we need to ask someone to forgive us, we should do it now. We need to live the present moment responsibly and joyfully and turn the future over to God. It belongs to God anyway."

This gem of wisdom so touched me that I enlisted Malcolm and other friends (and their associates) to share their thoughts on receiving a better life. One of the most moving responses came from a woman in her seventies who lives on a pension of less than $400 per month, yet considers herself rich. A moving force behind Habitat for Humanity and other projects in her community, she gave my friend, Bob Mullinax, her daily REA recipe for a better life:

REAd something worth reading.

REAch out to someone, other than family.

REAch up to a higher power.

cREAte something—a letter or other writing, even something as small as a pan of biscuits or a patch on your blue jeans.

REAlize your blessings, to discourage the materialistic desire for more, and to promote thanksgiving for life.

REAssess. What changes would improve your life, in your job, your schedule, and your relationships?

Debra Murphy, a professor at Duke University's Divinity School replied, "When I think about what it means to live well,

I'm reminded over and over that the 'good life' is one that must be emulated and imitated—we learn to live well by observing others and modeling our own lives after their example. So, if [a] better life can be achieved only by patterning one's existence after moral exemplars, it's important to recognize the significance of community and friendship."[2]

In chapter 1, I mentioned observations about being comfortable with oneself, which came from Bob's son, Marc Mullinax. Here is the conclusion of his message: "Our level of comfort plays a huge part in how we view the world and understand its operations. No one is mature save that they are free of anxiety and know the comfort for which they were made or intended.

"I'm not talking about 'cold comfort,' or the escaping of responsibilities that our drive to be comfortable can induce. After all, a year of being comfortable can wear down one's rage over injustice, make one obese, and generally make a person without care. Moreover, the Divine does not dawdle in the comfortable zone.... Too much comfortableness leads to stagnant faith, held together with fear, fear that none of this comfort...was meant for me."

THE BLESSING OF SOLITUDE

The quest for a better life consumes millions. That is, they worry constantly about making it through life. In compiling notes for this book, my assistant ran a check on an Internet search engine for "worry" and came up with 500,000 entries. The inquiry was prompted by a *Time* magazine cover story about understanding anxiety. Both are indicators that worry runs rampant in our society, bringing with it the consequences of poor health, dissatisfaction, unhappiness, and lack of productivity. We can literally worry ourselves to death.

I wish I could say I am immune from this habit. I should be after surviving numerous crises in my life and seeing that few were as bad as I had feared. I will never forget (nor do I care to repeat) the scene outside my home as the young father of two children. As a typical male—measuring my self-worth by money—I reached into my pocket and came up with two cents. At the time we didn't have a dime in the bank nor any idea of how we could make it until payday. That afternoon I received a check for a high school class I taught on a part-time basis, carrying us until I received my next paycheck. Ultimately, I had nothing to worry about.

But occasionally I lapse into fretting over something, most recently concerns about the future and what it holds for our children and grandchild. Questions drift through my mind. Will they make it? What kind of world will they live in? Things are changing so fast now; will they be able to cope? Will they be happy? If our economy falls apart, will they be able to make a living?

You may have noticed a common thread in the above questions: there is little I can do about any of them, just as I couldn't make money appear out of thin air as a young father. This is a good illustration of the foolishness of much of what we worry about. It reminds me of the sound bite that a fellow disc jockey in Charlotte used to punch up periodically for laughs, "A hundred years from now, what the heck difference will it make?"

Just because I have taken a positive, optimistic outlook within these pages, it does not mean that I do not recognize that life is hard and that people grapple with serious issues. No matter how you cut it, or how many facades people erect or phony masks they wear, life is a struggle. Yet overcoming struggles gives us wisdom, knowledge, and strength. As we battle, we must acknowledge that most of the potential troubles we worry over will never come to pass.

One antidote for worry is solitude. Solitude is the practiced, disciplined habit of withdrawing to pray, meditate on the good in our lives, and develop an appreciation for God's work in this world. A person who cultivates solitude can be content in the middle of a football stadium filled with 100,000 screaming fans.

Someone who insists on cramming his life with noise and empty activities can sit in the same stadium and feel dreadfully alone.

I think one reason solitude is a lost art today is because many people feel so lonely that they do not want to consciously remove themselves from everyone and be quiet. A pastoral counselor once told me that 99 percent of the problems he deals with stem from loneliness. I still remember the poll I once read in a church magazine where 80 percent of those interviewed admitted they were lonely. Doctors have called loneliness the culprit behind alcoholism, drug abuse, and psychosomatic illnesses.

Instead of getting bogged down in the negative side of aloneness, though, strive to see its positive side. Solitude can give you personal insights and provide you a strong sense of self. Michelangelo never would have painted the Sistine Chapel if he constantly needed other people's company. Because of his deafness, Thomas Edison mastered the light bulb and hundreds of other inventions. Jesus formulated his famous Sermon on the Mount during prayer and solitude.

If you use time alone to pursue meaningful disciplines, solitude can be like water to a budding flower. I first heard about solitude from Quaker writer Elton Trueblood, who described almost going crazy when he first sat quietly for an hour. But in the last two minutes of that hour, God spoke to him softly and gave him a resolve and a calm that lasted the rest of his life. As Psalm 46:10 says, "Be still and know that I am God."

Look around and you can see God at work: His hands crafted the Grand Canyon, Niagara Falls, and mountain ranges that spread across the Appalachians, the American West, and Alaska. In the stillness, if you wait patiently, you will hear Him. Turn off the cell phone, pager, TV, radio, and laptop computer and go to meet Him. Then receive all the life God has to offer.

Chapter 12

Step 12: Embrace the Future

SEVERAL YEARS AGO a kind benefactor telephoned Linda Morgan, the campus life director of one of our children's homes, with an offer of free T-shirts. However, the caller wanted assurances that the kids would get them. Charles Rector told her of offering similar gifts to other institutions, only to later discover that the intended recipients went shirtless. After delivering them, Linda sent a thank-you letter, along with notes of appreciation from the residents. That was not the end. Rector returned with more shirts.

The fourth time he showed up, in the autumn of 1998, he told Linda he wanted to share his story. Despite some pressing appointments, she stopped to listen. Rector told her of growing up in North Carolina and becoming a pastor at several churches in Virginia. One day he received a call asking him to come and help build a church in Madison County, North Carolina. After finishing the task, he preached in another small church. To earn extra income, he started an automobile business with another man. But this promising venture turned to dust when his partner embezzled all the funds, leaving him and his wife nearly penniless.

"In July of 1993, I went to bed with seven dollars in my pocket," he said. "I was fifty-seven years old. I prayed. Then I got up in the morning. The first time I gave you T-shirts, I sold over $10,000 in T-shirts the next two days. I have a booth at the farmers' market, and I had two buses pull in and buy T-shirts. I feel like God is telling me that I'm being blessed when I give to you.

"It's a miracle. In the past four years, I've sold over a million dollars in T-shirts. I'm able to have a home now. I want to do something for you. I can feel something special going on here. Every time I have come, you and other people here have been nice and helped me carry things and talked to me."

I love telling that story because it illustrates the final step in creating a worthwhile life. At an age when few people would have hired him, with his gut aching from the betrayal of a "Christian" business partner, Charles Rector easily could have given up and quit. He could have been like the people I have heard about over the years who suffer a reversal of fortune and escape into alcohol-laced self-pity for the rest of their days. Instead, Rector got up and embraced the future. Hoping to recover, and in spite of the unfairness and outrage of his circumstances, he moved ahead. And he did it one step at a time.

But he is not the only supporter I have known who took a steady gaze at the future and kept going. Though now deceased, Elbert Angel started using his scrap operation for noble purposes at the age of sixty. He would travel throughout the community, picking up tin cans, and load them on a tractor-trailer at his yard. When it was full, he would sell the load and bring us a check for several thousand dollars. He picked up cans for twenty years, not stopping until he reached eighty. Now you know why we still refer fondly to him as our "angel of mercy."

Or consider Pat McSwain, who hired me for one of my first radio jobs while I was still in high school. In the summer of 2002, he mailed me a copy of his self-published memoirs. In an accompanying letter, he noted that at ninety-three he still drives to a shopping mall every day to walk a mile or two. In his book, he tells of going to the doctor for a physical. Upon hearing his age, the doctor looked shocked and grabbed his chart to verify the truth.

"My children say even though they see less hair, more wrinkles, and a little slower movement, I don't seem to have aged past fifty," he writes. "That's certainly how I feel. I continue to read several newspapers and magazines, with CNN running on the television in the background…I have no aches and pains, and other than continuing to miss my wife a lot, I am very happy.

"I really enjoy being involved with my children, grandchildren and great-grandchildren. Almost every weekend I'm doing something with some of them. Maybe someday when I get old I'll start to slow down, but for now I'm happy to be 'on hold' at fifty."[1]

Clinging to Fear

Some people refuse to embrace the future, a sad, regrettable choice. I still remember reading about a woman who lived in destitute conditions, picking up clothes at the Salvation Army, begging door-to-door for food, and finally wasting away at a nursing home as a pitiful, emaciated shadow. But after her death, authorities discovered she had left behind more than a million dollars, including $800,000 in cash and several hundred shares of valuable stock, stored in two safety deposit boxes.

Though a much smaller nest egg, another example of failing to live with an eye on the future comes from a bequest made to our organization more than a decade ago. It involved the estate of John Duncan, a man who did not trust the government or banks. When he could not persuade his friend, Bob Lotz, to take $8,000 of the cash he had accumulated, he declared he would bury the money and did not care if it was ever found.

When Duncan, who had never married, died he left us all his possessions. Appointed the estate's executor, Lotz spent more than a year looking for them. True to his word, Duncan had squirreled away his cash. The only easy find was $46.45, which Lotz located the day of his friend's death. From there he started removing doors, window trim, and electrical wall outlet plates, and searching every nook imaginable. Three days later he found more than $2,000 beneath a potato bin. Then he returned a few days a week for months, usually leaving empty-handed.

Finally, frustrated that he had not located the main cache, Lotz prayed, "Look, God, you know I'm honest. I tried looking. I'm tired of looking for this money. I shouldn't have to go through all this. Please let me find it. You know I'll turn every cent in; it's for a good cause."

On his next excursion into the woodshed, he noticed a plastic medicine tube against the foundation and a Wheaties box containing $1,580. He returned to the pump house, studying the thick concrete walls and removing the roof. This time he found four plastic bags with a total of $7,000. A couple months later he found eighteen $100 bills in a peanut butter jar in a hog house. In the rafters above was a tobacco tin with seven more. Total cash discoveries came to just over $13,000.[2]

Though these are extreme examples, it is too easy to cluck, "What fools!" while overlooking the ways in which we cling to fear. Is choosing "stability" actually casting a vote for boredom? Or "prudently" piling up ever-larger retirement accounts in reality dreading that some old-age disease will suck away our life savings? Is a refusal to share with those who are less fortunate a reflection that we do not think there will be any more to replace what we give away? Only you can answer these questions truthfully as you search your heart.

ENJOYING LIFE

What these stories show is that some *enjoy* life. Others *endure* it. In which category do you fall? Truthfully, all of us are seeking direction. Most of us need help at one time or another during our lives. All of us have missed intersections and have taken wrong turns. Fortunately, we have not been left on our own to deal with life's unexpected wrinkles. We have two precious resources to help guide our steps.

The first is experience. We do not have to plow fresh ground constantly. We can stand on our predecessors' shoulders. Each generation does not have to discover anew the law of gravity, invent the light bulb, or design engines from scratch. And, in a broader sense, the lessons of history are there to speak to us—if we will listen.

President Harry Truman will always have a special footnote in history as the president who authorized the dropping of the first atomic bomb. In light of the unbelievable disasters of Hiroshima and Nagasaki, the immense loss of life, and gruesome deformities among the children who survived, historians continue to debate the advisability of this destruction (though always with the benefit of hindsight).

Regardless of how you feel, we can say we learned a costly lesson. And, this pair of bombings have prevented other bombings. The horror the world witnessed in 1945 has been a deterrent to the use of nuclear weapons, even though those old weapons do not compare to the destructive capabilities of today's arsenal. Yet our fear is so great, and rightly so, that protests greeted the government's decision to ship waste materials through many states en route to their final repository at Yucca Mountain, Nevada.

Likewise, the Nazi ovens of Auschwitz and Dachau, and their attendant Holocaust, taught us a lesson about uncontrolled hatred. Sadly, it was not etched permanently in people's minds. Some revisionists deny the horror even happened. In addition, the creation of Israel in 1948 fanned continuing anti-Semitic fervor, which is seen most graphically in the Israeli-Palestinian conflict.

Secondly, and on a smaller scale, we carry the lessons of personal history. We learn the folly of rediscovering old territory. When we experience a nasty bout of indigestion, we shun the foods that caused it. When we know what causes our allergies to flare up, we stay away from the source of swelling and sneezing. Remembering the times when we lost our temper should help us to avoid such situations, hopefully developing a more patient nature as we mature.

But experience is not enough. We also need expectation. Though we can recall the past, we must be able to anticipate the future. We spend numerous years getting educated in hopes of finding a good job. We follow a diet for weeks or months, keeping our eye on a trimmer figure. We spend hours at the keyboard, harvesting excellence at the piano. The effort is worth it because of expectation. Take that away and the present would lock us up in a blue funk.

Everyone needs to find something in life to look forward to, to anticipate. We make a mistake if we think it has to be a trip to the Bahamas or a vacation in Hawaii. It could be welcoming home a child from college or watching your grandchild march in the homecoming parade. We all need to learn to find value in anticipating small events and learn how to make them special.

Enjoy life or endure it. I much prefer the first option. Keeping an eye on the future is one way of walking the more pleasant path. As you go, here is my checklist of ways that can help you march ahead:

1. Have a purpose in life. Staying busy is a sure antidote to boredom and early death.

2. Know that things generally work out for the best, even though it may be hard to see how, especially when you are dealing with the loss of a spouse, child, parent, or friend.

3. Maintain a positive outlook. If you look for the good in people and circumstances, you are more likely to find it.

4. Learn something new every day, or week, or month. We are never too old to learn. Put another way, you really can teach an old dog new tricks.

5. Find something you are passionate about and then do it.

6. Remember you were placed on this earth for a reason. We are only on this stage of life for a short time, so make the most of your opportunities.

7. Remember the MED formula for a long life: Meditation, Exercise, and Diet. Prayer, staying active, and watching what you eat promote good health.

8. Here is one I credit to the late Jim Valvano, the exuberant basketball coach at North Carolina State University: find something to laugh about every day and find something to cry about every day. God gave you emotions. Use them.

9. Make a firm decision regarding a possible course of action. After you have made that commitment, take the first step. Always look ahead, never behind.

10. Do everything with great enthusiasm. I wrote a short prayer to illustrate this point: "Lord, my times are in Your hands. Help me be faithful to the duty of the present moment."

Folks, the choice is yours. You can find riches beyond measure and create a life worth living but only if you embrace the future.

NOTES

··· Chapter 1 ···

Step 1: Accept Yourself

1. James Michener, *The Fires of Spring* (New York: Random House, 1949), 488.

2. Paul Tournier, *The Meaning of Persons* (New York and Evanston, IL: Harper & Row, 1957), 47–48.

3. My thanks to Marc Mullinax, a professor at Mars Hill College in North Carolina, for sharing his "comfort" insights with me (2003).

··· Chapter 3 ···

Step 3: Be a Friend

1. John MacArthur, *The MacArthur New Testament Commentary: Ephesians* (Chicago, IL: Moody Press, 1986), 78.

2. Robert D. Putnam, *Bowling Alone: The Collapse and Revival of American Community* (New York: Simon & Schuster, 2001).

3. Claude S. Fischer, "Network Analysis and Urban Studies," in *Networks and Places: Social Relations in the Urban Setting* (New York: Free Press, 1977), quoted in Robert D. Putnam, *Bowling Alone: The Collapse and Revival of American Community* (New York: Simon and Schuster, 1990), 20.

4. Peggy Noonan, *What I Saw at the Revolution* (New York: Random House, 1990), 38.

5. Ellen Goodman, "Didn't We Have Fun?" *The Louisville Courier-Journal*, 15 March 2002.

··· Chapter 4 ···

Step 4: Love Abundantly

1. *Charity & Children*, December 1995. Published by The Baptist Children's Homes of North Carolina, Thomasville, NC.

··· Chapter 6 ···

Step 6: Remember Nature's Nurture

1. John Killinger, *Bread for the Wilderness, Wine for the Journey* (Waco, TX: Word Books, 1976), 75.

··· Chapter 7 ···

Step 7: Seek Uplifting People

1. Millard Fuller quoted by Tim Stafford, "How to Build Homes Without Putting Up Walls," *Christianity Today*, 10 June 2002, 31.

2. Ivor H. Evans, *Brewer's Dictionary of Phrase and Fable*, 14th ed. (Great Britain: Cassell Publishers, Ltd., 1989), 414.

··· Chapter 9 ···

Step 9: Be a Mentor

1. Zig Ziglar, *Zig: The Autobiography of Zig Ziglar* (New York: Doubleday, 2002), 143.

··· Chapter 11 ···

Step 11: Receive Life

1. Lynn Johnston, "For Better or Worse," 21 May 2002: United Media.

2. Debra Murphy, personal correspondence.

··· Chapter 12 ···

Step 12: Embrace the Future

1. Personal letter to the author, August 6, 2002.

2. An account of this incident originally appeared in the September 1993 issue of *Charity & Children*, our organization's monthly newsletter.

Contact Information

Dr. Michael Blackwell
Baptist Children's Homes
P.O. Box 338
Thomasville, NC 27361-0338
Web site: www.bchfamily.org
E-mail: mcblackwell@bchfamily.org

Ken Walker
1355 Bardstown Rd. #217
Louisville, KY 40204-1353
Web site: www.kenwalker.biz
E-mail: kenwalker33@cs.com